LET'S BACK UP A BIT

CONVERSATIONS WITH PIONEERING KIWI CHRISTIAN MUSICIANS

★ ★ ★ ★ BRETT WILSON ★ ★ ★ ★

Castle

Let's Back Up a Bit
Published by Brett Wilson
with Castle Publishing Ltd
New Zealand

© 2020 Brett Wilson

ISBN 978-0-473-53464-6 (Softcover)
ISBN 978-0-473-53465-3 (ePUB)
ISBN 978-0-473-53466-0 (Kindle)

Editing:
Marie Anticich

Production & Typesetting:
Andrew Killick
Castle Publishing Services
www.castlepublishing.co.nz

Cover Design:
Karl Berzins

Scriptures taken from
the Holy Bible, New International Version®, NIV®.
Copyright © 1973, 1978, 1984, 2011 by Biblica, Inc.™
Used by permission of Zondervan.
All rights reserved worldwide.

ALL RIGHTS RESERVED

No part of this publication may be reproduced,
stored in a retrieval system, or transmitted
in any form or by any means, electronic, mechanical,
photocopying, recording or otherwise,
without prior written permission from the author.

LET'S BACK UP A BIT

ACKNOWLEDGEMENTS

Special thanks to God (the ultimate Creator); Pam, Dylan and Ella Wilson; Mum and Dad (for tolerating the music coming out of my tape deck in the '80s); Ross Wilson and Ross Dickey (for feeding new music into my tape deck in the '80s); Jan Rodgers (nee Wilson) (for helping me decipher the lyrics coming out of my tape deck in the '80s).

Also thanks to Vision College, Ray Pickett, Joanne Whitt, Caleb Driver, Simon Moetara, Jon Clarke, Andrew Killick (Castle Publishing), Marie Anticich, Jenny Horst, Karl Berzins, Jen Spicer, Steve and Cheryl Hamilton, Goff Van't Hof, Mark de Jong, Jon E. Clist, and all of the Christian bands and musicians in New Zealand, whether they're mentioned in this book or not.

CONTENTS

Intro	9
Dave White (The Revs)	19
Derek Lind	59
David & Dale Garratt	99
Steve Apirana	121
Stephen Bell-Booth	155
Phil Joel	179
Hoi Polloi	215
Outro	259
About the Author	264

INTRO

The Jesus Movement of the late 1960s and early 1970s resulted in a significant number of young people around the globe converting to Christianity. Some of these young people were musicians who began writing songs in the style of the music they knew best, rock & roll, but often with a Christian message. This new music was uncharted territory for the church to deal with and was eventually labelled 'contemporary Christian music' (CCM).

Because the music sounded the same as secular music, many church leaders deemed it ungodly, and thought putting Christian lyrics to 'worldly' music was sacrilegious. But music is just notes, chords and beats. G on the guitar is neither sacred nor worldly. It's just G.

So it was the style of the music that offended some of the church leaders. Perhaps they preferred hymns? Maybe they didn't realise that the tunes for many hymns came from drinking songs in public houses? No doubt this would've upset some people at the time, but, as Larry Norman used to sing, 'Why should the devil have all the good music?'

Norman is generally considered the father of CCM who, along with Randy Stonehill, Chuck Girard and Petra, to name a few, paved the way for a new generation of Christian musicians, while facing criticism from more conservative voices within the church.

Let's Back Up a Bit

The controversy didn't wane even when it was clear that many Christian artists' songs contained lyrics of explicit faith or evangelistic messages urging listeners to repent and be 'saved'. It didn't seem to matter to CCM's detractors that people were repenting and being saved through the music.

I was born in 1973 when the Jesus Movement was in full swing, particularly in America. Just as New Zealand swooned to Elvis shaking his pelvis in the 1950s, we also felt the effects of the spiritual awakening shaking the USA's west coast in the early 1970s.

Like many other kids, I began showing an interest in music around the age of ten. It started with an obsession with Michael Jackson, whose recently released magnum-opus album, *Thriller*, became the biggest selling album of all time. Funnily enough, I memorised the lyrics to the title track without really knowing how the music went (a kid at school had given me a copy of the printed lyrics).

Considering it contained horror themes, I felt immense guilt at reciting those lyrics. I didn't dare ask my parents to buy the record for me, knowing full well such music would not be allowed in the house. Fair enough. It was 1984 and I was only ten years old; it certainly wasn't sanctified music. My guilt was intensified when a family friend, Uncle Doug, told me off when he caught me watching the famous 13-minute video clip. I learned that day that zombies and werewolves were off limits.

In an ironic twist, the first album I ever owned was *We Are the World* (1985), the big charity song for Africa co-written by Michael Jackson. When I asked Mum to buy me the record for Christmas, I made sure she knew it wasn't Christian music. The fact that she seemed to not care made me wonder if the family had given up the faith altogether!

I started piano lessons when I was seven. I'd hop on my

Cruiser and bike to Mrs Rive's house every week and learn the classics such as 'Ten Little Indians' and 'C Major Scale'. Good times. But after three years I gave up because I didn't want to practice. Not when there were better things to do like watching the *The Smurfs* on TV.

When I was 11, my dad and I began learning the organ together for about four years, where we were treated to even better classics such as 'A Whiter Shade of Pale'. The organ taught me about melody (right hand), chords (left hand) and bass (left foot). Today, I'm a multi-instrumentalist and a practitioner of music with a Master of Arts degree and have spent half my life teaching music, and so I'm grateful for my parents' encouragement to stick with the lessons.

Growing up, I remember we had a stereo unit in the lounge, but I don't recall a lot of records being played. I had seen though not heard, a certain non-Christian record by the George Baker Selection. I remember being a little bit frightened by the album cover photo as it featured males with long hair. They looked a bit like Black Sabbath, but now I realise the music was kind of easy-listening country music, particularly Mum's favourite track 'Baby Blue'.

If music was played in the house – aside from Dad's alarm clock radio – *Come on Ring Those Bells* by the Christian singer, Evie, was the soundtrack to our Christmases. One author claims Evie was 'widely regarded as one of the most beautiful women in the world...'* though I'd like to see the paperwork on that research.

Even more commonly played were records by the American televangelist Jimmy Swaggart. Some might remember him more for his moral lapse and his infamous confession on TV

---

* Mark Allan Powell, *Encyclopedia of Contemporary Christian Music* (Peabody: Hendrickson Publishers, 2002), 312.

Let's Back Up a Bit

in 1988. It's fair to say my parents were big Swaggart fans, certainly pre-scandal.

When we went on long trips, Dad often played Swaggart's music on the car tape deck. Jimmy certainly had catchy tunes but, more importantly, for me, he tore it up on the piano. Fittingly, his cousin is Jerry Lee Lewis, the wild 1950s rock & roll singer/pianist renowned for his hit song, 'Great Balls of Fire'.

But the irony of being brought up on this music is that Swaggart was outspoken against rock & roll, Christian or secular; the kind of music I eventually grew to love. Swaggart represented many from his generation who believed rock music was a tool of the devil used to lure young people away from their faith and, as such, Christians shouldn't listen to it. Southern Gospel music? Sure! Fill your boots! Rock & roll? Absolutely not!

It's one thing to dislike a certain type of music but it's another thing to label that style 'evil'. Nevertheless, it was preachers like Swaggart who convinced many parents that this indeed was the case. My parents may have felt some tension here but, thankfully, they tolerated CCM enough for me to enjoy Christian rock music.

In retrospect, I sometimes feel a twinge of envy at musicians who grew up listening to popular music. I've read countless stories of famous musicians who talk about listening to, say, the Beatles or the Rolling Stones, or perhaps cool jazz records by Miles Davis.

I often wonder if such stories are exaggerated, and if they simply don't mention the 'uncool' music they listened to like the Bay City Rollers or the Wombles. While I heard bits and pieces on the radio, it was generally something our household avoided.

I would try to watch the Top 40 countdown show, *Ready to*

Roll, every Saturday to see who was at number one but if Dad walked in he would say, 'What's this rubbish?!' and I'd have to change the channel. That's good parenting though, Dad. Thanks for helping me be rubbish-free since '73.

Courtesy of my big brother's growing cassette tape collection, my soundtrack for the summer of '86 was Bob Dylan's second gospel album, *Saved* (1980). Although it was one of his most critically panned albums, it was one of my favourites. 'What Can I Do For You?' contains arguably his best harmonica playing and the bass riff on 'Solid Rock' blew my 12-year-old mind. At that time, I had no idea that Dylan, who was clearly suggesting that the answers to life's questions are found in Jesus, was more famous decades earlier for singing 'the answer is blowin' in the wind!'

About a year later, the CCM band Petra changed everything for me. *This Means War!* was *the* album to own if you were a teenaged-Christian in 1987. It ticked all the boxes in terms of what was deemed mandatory for Christian hard rock (yeah, it was hard rock back then); distorted guitars, vocals that seemed limitless in the high range, big snare drums, fast keyboard runs, power ballads and, of course, lyrics that were mini-sermons backed up with scriptural references.

Soon afterwards, this American band announced a concert in Auckland, a 90-minute drive from my hometown of Hamilton. Petra was my first concert ever, and I even ended up taking home the drummer's drumstick. We were sitting in the balcony of Auckland's Town Hall, overlooking the stage, and after the concert, I leaned over and yelled, 'Hey, Louie! Can I have a drumstick?' He said, 'Sure,' and tossed one up to me. Ask, and it will be given. I've still got the drumstick. Kept it in my office for years and showed it to my music students when we talked about Petra and CCM.

By this time, I was going to high school and realised it wasn't cool to admit I grew up on Jimmy Swaggart's music (not that anyone knew who he was, which is kind of the point). It became equally embarrassing to admit that Petra were my 'Beatles' or, for a closer association, my 'Def Leppard'.

As Bob Dylan sang, 'The Times are A-Changin' and they certainly have changed. Nowadays kids can go online and instantly see their favourite musician's latest haircut. But when I was a teen, it was hard to even find a photo of your favourite Christian musician. This resulted in some confusion when I first saw Petra in concert. I'd only ever seen one photo of the group on the back of a record, and I mistakenly identified the guy standing in the middle as the vocalist, John Schlitt. I learned at the concert that he was actually the keyboardist. I mean, who puts the keyboardist in the middle?! Hearing that famous voice come out of the 'wrong' person was akin to seeing a radio DJ for the first time and thinking, 'They're not supposed to look like that!' Younger people these days are less likely to experience that freaky thing.

Arguably, seeing a musician perform live on stage in those days was more special than today when you can simply stream your favourite artist online. Back then, musicians seemed to be untouchable, unreachable and mysterious, compared to today's immediate accessibility. And I'm sure that added to the thrill.

Over the next few years, I attended shows by Christian rock bands such as Stryper, Whitecross and Rez Band. Stryper (who, ironically, were saved through Swaggart's ministry) were particularly controversial for their androgynous costumes and makeup. But by the 1990s, tours by famous Christian international groups seemed to have dried up, perhaps in favour of playing at Parachute, the burgeoning Christian festival.

On the local scene, Derek Lind, Steve Apirana, Stephen Bell-

Booth, the Revs, Hoi Polloi, and Drinkwater are just a few names notable for producing music akin to that of their American or British counterparts. Some of these Kiwi artists wrote songs that contained a socio-political message; others contained sermonettes from Scripture, or a declaration of devotion to Christ. Other artists just wanted to make music without succumbing to 'worldly' messages in their lyrics. For many audiences, their music was a safer alternative to secular rock music.

While some of these Kiwi musicians attempted international success, they were mainly limited to the local music scene. This is nothing to be scorned at. In fact, these musicians arguably inspired and influenced future generations of Kiwi musicians more than international Christian musicians, simply because of the notion, 'If *they* can do it, maybe *I* can do it.' This was certainly the case for me and, no doubt, for other musicians.

The importance of Youth for Christ (YFC) on the New Zealand music scene cannot be over-expressed here. From the 1970s through to the 1990s, YFC's monthly rallies, held in the main centres and in some smaller towns, were the most significant event for exposing new Christian musicians to young people across the country. This applied to me personally and I enjoyed being introduced to, say, the Taranaki Boys and the Revs one month, Derek Lind and Guy Wishart the next, and so on.

These acts would be interspersed with comedy routines and skits, often acted out by my friends or acquaintances through church circles. The concerts would always finish with a sermon, often resulting in dozens of young people accepting Jesus Christ as their Saviour.

Post-rally gigs were often staged at a venue or café to allow audiences to hear more songs from the guest artists. YFC also put on other gigs that were less evangelistic and just an excuse for bands to play and for young people to gather in an abandoned warehouse or similar and enjoy the entertainment.

It must be pointed out that radio did not play a significant part in exposing this music. Radio Rhema was mainly for grown-ups, and the youth-oriented Life FM wasn't invented yet. Also, some of these artists couldn't afford to record an album in a recording studio anyway, and so this made getting to live gigs a higher priority (this was long before the days of doing it yourself in Pro-Tools on your laptop). To experience these musicians, you had to go to the gig and sometimes there wasn't even an album to play, let alone a video to watch; there certainly wasn't a website to visit or updates to follow on social media.

Beginning in the early 1970s, YFC also instigated touring ministry teams. Every year auditionees would be selected to tour New Zealand, playing at high schools during the week and at evening concerts in the local school or town hall. These shows weren't too dissimilar to the local YFC rallies but, due to selecting the best musicians nationwide, and the months of training and rehearsals, the quality was potentially higher.

The two touring teams – Certain Sounds and Y-ONE – developed a reputation for putting on high-quality music and drama shows, with a punchy sermon to finish. Just as at local YFC rallies, droves of young people would respond to the invitation to receive Christ. These touring teams may have initially performed mostly Christian cover songs but, interestingly, this seemed to slowly shift to secular covers over time.

I can attest to this change of emphasis, being a regular YFC rally attendee in my youth, and also as a band member with Certain Sounds in 1994 (discussed further in the next chapter).

Songs were carefully chosen and usually contained a safe or wholesome message. They may not have been 'Christian' songs, but the lyrics were appropriated for a Christian message. For example, Lenny Kravitz' 'Are You Gonna Go My Way?' was implied as 'God's way'. Imagine the reaction from the likes of Jimmy Swaggart knowing that a Christian band was not only playing 'evil' rock music to spread the Gospel, but *secular* rock music!

Initially, for many musicians, CCM was a tool for ministry and evangelism. But as time went by other Christian musicians emerged with lyrics that could potentially appeal to a broader audience with songs that referred to Jesus as 'Him' or 'You', or by singing about day-to-day issues from the perspective of a believer.

By the early 1990s, it was more common for the music to be more of an artistic expression, and the message – if there was one at all – was more universal in its appeal, rather than an explicit message regarding the Christian faith. For example, a band like Drinkwater singing a message that can be summed up as 'Chill out Brussel Sprout!' would likely have been unheard of in CCM during the 1970s and 1980s.

Now, to explain my reasons for writing this book. The first reason is to examine the cultural shift in 'Christian' music from the 1970s through to the 1990s, with particular regard to pioneering Kiwi musicians. Their personal insights of the gradual change in music through the decades, and other anecdotes recounted in the following pages, will be revealing.

The second reason is to acknowledge these pioneers and to provide a voice for their stories, achievements and legacy. It would have been great to include so many more musicians who were important to Christian music in New Zealand. My apologies to those who aren't mentioned. This book is not a historical record but a 'snapshot' in which the musicians selected represent a host of others whose stories will be more or less similar.

Let's Back Up a Bit

So let's take a trip down Memory Lane as I chat to some of the interesting and talented Christian artists this country has produced.

DAVE WHITE (THE REVS)

Dave White has to be the most creative person I have ever met. He's not one to conform to the norm or to accept mediocrity. When I was in my early teens his reputation as guitarist for the Revs went before him.

I think a lot of people who witnessed the Revs live would agree they were probably the 'coolest' band around. 'Cool' can mean a few different things, particularly to do with music. For example, it's kind of cool that the guys in Coldplay get to play music together, but everything about the Strokes is *Cool* with a capital C. I reckon it was the latter kind of *Cool* that the Revs had.

As a teenager, I developed enough skills on the harmonica to turn heads and, more importantly, to get some gigs. Dave must have heard me play around 1991 as part of an acoustic duo I was in called Holy Smoke. He asked me to play at the odd YFC rally.

I had attended and loved those youth rallies, so that was a big deal for me. For a 17-year-old to play at Hamilton's Founders Theatre, a much humbler version of Carnegie Hall, before an audience of 1,200 or so … I had made it as a musician!

This led to an invitation from Dave, a few years later, to tour New Zealand and Western Australia in an outreach band run by YFC called Certain Sounds. It would be Dave's second time round as he had previously toured as the guitarist in 1988. This time

Let's Back Up a Bit

DAVE WHITE (PHOTO CREDIT: SIMON travaglia).

he was going to be road manager, bass player and preacher, and I was hired mainly for keyboard duties, but I got to play other instruments and sang a few songs as well.

As discussed in the Intro, Certain Sounds had been operating since the early 1970s, each year changing the band members who auditioned for a coveted spot. Y-ONE was another brand of the same sort of thing, though as well as Top 40 music, they included dance and drama. Each band was identified by the year in which they toured. My one was called Certain Sounds '94, and it was here where I was quickly introduced to Dave's creative way of thinking. Dave mashed-up songs long before anyone knew what a 'mash-up' was. 'Jesus Loves Me, This I Know' set to 'Blame It on the Boogie' *shouldn't* work, but he made it work.

I was honoured to be invited into Certain Sounds by the

Dave White (The Revs)

famous Dave White of the Revs fame. We became good friends during the tour and remain in regular contact to this day, often playing together in some sort of project of his. It is because of Dave that I have become a fellow bandmate with several interviewees in this book. And it is for this reason that I have placed Dave's interview as chapter one.

The Revs did not appear first in the continuum of Christian rock music in New Zealand, but they were among the first for me as a young bloke, and I have Dave to thank for the gigs that he's given me and also for introducing me to other great musicians, some of whom appear in this book.

In 2006, Dave put together the Bob Dylan Electric Gospel Band. Perhaps the name gives it away that this band paid tribute to the three gospel albums that Bob Dylan released decades ago. I was hired for keyboard/harmonica/vocal duties.

The line-up of this band was interchangeable. The first drummer was Bruce Parker, later replaced by Kevin Adair. Vernon Rive took over bass duties from Tim Trenwith. A.J. Bell was always on shared guitar and vocal duties. (I remembered Vernon and A.J.'s band from the late 1980s called the Yahoos.)

Dave also sang and played guitar as did the most famous guy in the band, Derek Lind (see his chapter for more). The Bob Dylan Electric Gospel Band was only supposed to do a one-off gig at Parachute Festival 2007, but a few years later we were still at it, gigging sporadically.

This band morphed into Country Drag; the concept of which was to cover famous Christian songs dressed in country music. While it was a fairly collaborative project, it was largely led by A.J. The line-up was similar to those already mentioned, but with Michael Te Young on drums and Glenn Ross Campbell added on pedal steel.

Glenn was, by far, the most experienced out of all of us, having gained international popularity in the late 1960s with bands such as the Misunderstood and Juicy Lucy. He used to hang with Jimi Hendrix and he played in Joe Cocker's band, just to name two legends! True story. And now he gets to play alongside me! That joke is stolen from Derek Lind's stage banter... that's quality banter!

A natural progression from Country Drag was the third incarnation of the band, the Redemption Highway Collective, a concept dreamed up by Derek's manager and close friend, Steve Hamilton (whom we all call 'Albert' in reference to Bob Dylan's manager, Albert Grossman). The concept was to play old gospel tunes in an alt-country or Americana style. The Collective also featured many of the same personnel, though with Andrew Horst on bass joined by his wife Jenny Horst on vocals (both of Hoi Polloi fame).

Also joining the Redemption Highway Collective was Guy Wishart whose album *Another Day in Paradise* I had purchased on cassette and adored as a 16-year-old. Steve and Ainsley Apirana also featured, along with Kevin Adair's wife Darlene Adair on vocals. Sadly, Darlene passed away in 2019. I recommend searching for her recording of 'Just Let Me Say' by Geoff Bullock or her duet with Stephen Bell-Booth on 'God Will Provide'. She had an astonishing voice.

The Redemption Highway Collective was a *large* band. If someone couldn't make it the gig would likely still go ahead, hence the word 'Collective' in the band name, I guess. That's also a lot of musicians whom I had grown up listening to and admiring as a teen. Thanks Dave! The latest incarnation of the band is the Lind-Apirana Blues Explosion... I wonder how long this is gonna go on for?!

In this chapter, Dave often talks about the Revs in a self-deprecating manner. He says, 'Vocally we were rubbish,' 'We were

Dave White (The Revs)

THE REDEMPTION HIGHWAY COLLECTIVE (2013)
FROM LEFT: GLENN R. CAMPBELL, GUY WISHART (ON RED CAR), A.J. BELL, ME (ON TRIKE), ANDREW HORST, KEVIN & DARLENE ADAIR, DEREK LIND (ON TRIKE), STEVE & AINSLEY APIRANA. ABSENT: DAVE WHITE & JENNY HORST. (PHOTO CREDIT: STEVE HAMILTON)

just learning to play,' 'We were song destructors ... twisting other people's ideas.' But he also mentions that the band had a 'high level of originality and creativity', and he has carried this high level of creativity through to every post-Revs project, such as the bands previously mentioned, as well as through other art forms such as Stations of the Cross (an Easter-themed art exhibition) and Trees at the Meteor (a Christmas-themed art exhibition).

Dave is a qualified high school teacher and legend has it that he once distributed marked assessments to his students dressed up as Santa Claus. One episode I witnessed first-hand was when I invited him to speak to my own group of tertiary students about his favourite artist of all-time, Bob Dylan.

At one point Dave cordoned off his teaching space with police tape like a crime scene and, donning ear muffs and safety glasses, announced to the students, 'This is what Bob Dylan did to mainstream music!' as he proceeded to take a chainsaw to a very thick book. With all the noise and mess, I think those students are unlikely to forget that 'lecture' in a hurry.

Dave has also expressed his creativity through what he calls 'rants'. I think these may have started off as long but cleverly worded emails to those on his Rolodex in an attempt to drum-up support for whatever project he was plugging at the time. After a while this led to a weekly stint on local radio ranting about topical issues, and he has ranted at weddings and bar mitzvahs all over the place.

Dave's the kind of guy to get a little embarrassed about being the subject in a book but, through his creative output with the Revs, YFC, Incedo and other multiple projects, he would've made some kind of impact on thousands of New Zealanders. That's pretty impressive. Let the interview begin:

Brett Wilson: This book is about pioneers of new Christian music in New Zealand. How do you feel about being included in that?

Dave White: That's up to you, mate.

BW: You've got no opinion on that?

DW: Are we recording?

Dave White (The Revs)

BW: Yeah. The interview has started... and we're off to a rollicking start!

DW: [Laughter – long awkward pause] Well, yeah it did seem that there was an emergent kind of thing, when I was young, to play rock & roll under a kind of 'Jesus' umbrella. It felt a bit radical, I suppose, at times.

BW: There weren't a lot of people doing that at the time?

DW: Um... yeah. There were bands all around the country when we started but it was still looked upon as the devil's music, you know?

BW: Yeah, I remember that a lot.

DW: There was a little bit of scepticism around what you were doing and how you were doing it. We played at pubs also, so that was interesting.

BW: Doubly bad?

DW: Doubly bad, yeah!

BW: Your upbringing was probably quite similar to mine, which is bound to have an influence on the music you listened to. Can you think of any music that was allowed or not allowed in your home?

DW: Yeah, yeah. I remember winning an art competition and the prize was the *Sgt. Pepper's Lonely Hearts Club Band* LP. I thought I was getting the Peter Frampton, Bee Gees 1970s version, but it was the Beatles' original. But for some reason it disappeared for years. Later to be found hidden in the old man's wardrobe. [Laughter] So yeah. That left town for years, never to be seen.

BW: Wow. What did your parents listen to?

DW: They had three secular albums: Neil Diamond, the Carpenters' *Greatest Hits* and... [long pause] I can't remember the third one. Maybe there was just two? The rest of it was Christian classics: Evie, the Continental Singers. I saw the Continentals live every year. Sensational. They also had Robert Colman, from Australia. He's the father of the other Colman guy... Colman Trio...

BW: Paul Colman.

DW: Yeah. So the stereo really only got turned up on Sundays. The rest of the time, it was pretty quiet. But the breakthrough for me was picking up a couple of 45s at a St. John's College garage sale. The Beatniks... Johnny and the Beatniks or something. It was kind of weird rock & roll. Don't quote me on that. I found the single just the other day.

BW: You've still got it?

DW: Well, not the same single but the song.

BW: Do you remember the name of the song?

DW: [Long pause] No.

It turns out the band was Johnny and the Hurricanes, and the song

Dave White (The Revs)

was 'Beatnik Fly'. Listening to it now, I would describe it as early '60s surf music with a pre-school melody played on organ!

BW: Would you say secular music was frowned upon in your house, or is that a bit harsh?

DW: Well, in my household it was never overtly discussed. But just because of the breadth of the record collection, it was all Christian stuff, you grow up with that kind of slant or bias. But then there was the youth group influence. We had books, American books about anti-rock stuff. They listed all the artists that you couldn't listen to: the Eagles, Elton John...

BW: By Bob Larson?

This evangelist may have later softened his stance towards rock music but I mention him because he wrote a number of books warning Christians of the dangers of rock & roll, as did Jimmy Swaggart and, perhaps most militantly, Jeff Godwin.

DW: Bob Larson. That's the one. Even now, I find myself listening to 'Stairway to Heaven' and I can't really do it. You know? Because it was so appallingly evil. [Laughter]

BW: I have the same reaction!

DW: Even the Eagles' music is tainted when I listen to it.

BW: 'Hotel California'?

DW: Yeah. Anton LaVey in the window, I mean it's total rubbish!

Let's Back Up a Bit

This is a reference to the inside cover of Hotel California, which according to Jeff Godwin has an image of Anton LaVey, founder of the Church of Satan, peering down from a balcony.

DW: We had backward masking sessions...

Dave's referring to teaching videos that were played at youth groups, in which snippets of famous songs are played backwards to reveal evil messages. 'Another One Bites the Dust' by Queen is memorable for me as we were told the message when played backwards says, 'It's fun to smoke marijuana.' But if nobody told you this, all you're likely to hear is gibberish, so it's highly speculative.

The basic premise of all of this was that Satan was spreading subliminal messages that could be discerned only when the music was played backwards. Depending on my mood, I either laugh or cry at the thought of Christians going to the trouble of searching for these 'evil messages'. If this is all new to you, it's all online – go and have a few laughs (or shed some tears)... after reading this chapter though...

DW: I lost a lot of records and was very conscious of what I was listening to. I thought it was a little bit risqué when I stepped outside of the airwaves of the holy sanctum.

BW: So you were told to get rid of your records or...

DW: No, that was my own choice. But the youth group consensus was, you know... I remember people driving over their cassettes on the road outside youth group meetings. Pretty sad. Pretty sad times really. A lot of good music went down. [Laughter]

I remember hiring the keys to a church for the Revs' band rehearsal. The key was given with the agreement that we wouldn't be playing any rock & roll, whereupon we unleashed

Dave White (The Revs)

Iron Maiden's 'Number of the Beast' as our opening number, just to break that rule. [Laughter]

BW: I went and saw Iron Maiden earlier this year.

DW: Oh, wow. How was that?

BW: Yeah, it was fine. I'm not a huge fan. In fact, I think part of the reason I went was out of rebellion towards all this stuff that was fed to us growing up, you know? They're phenomenal musicians and I enjoyed that aspect of it and, just like many artists, they may have the odd lyric that I don't agree with and you dust it off your shoulder. But my question is, and this is not to condone everything under the sun, but where do you draw the line?

I guess what bugs me a bit is that music tends to get an unfair amount of focus in terms of whether it's 'good' or 'evil' much more than other mediums, at least it used to. I'm not aware of evangelists who have written books on secular movies or on secular books that we're not allowed to watch or read. Maybe we should try watching *The Godfather* backwards to see what the devil's got to say through that? Or how about we read *To Kill a Mockingbird* upside down while standing on our heads?

DW: Yeah! Fair comment. I think the travesty in our upbringing was the side-lining or even dismissal of the major tenets of Christ's teaching to these weird issues. I don't recall many Baptist sermons about non-violence. We didn't backward mask our incomes in order to have less flasher cars etc.

And it was pretty much a list of don'ts – the moral police – with less of a prophetic vision of what being active in the dream of God might look like. Hysteria around popular music and its evils was just bad, wimpy theology and 'small God' syndrome.

Let's Back Up a Bit

BW: Very well said. I've thought about it a fair amount, but I'm not sure if I can articulate it as well as you have. But it seems that the Jesus Movement brought about this new music; Larry Norman being the leader of the pack, Keith Green, Randy Stonehill, and this whole thing called CCM (contemporary Christian music) eventually developed.

You and I grew up in that time where people basically said, 'Okay, this is what you are allowed to listen to, and therefore you're not allowed to listen to that stuff.' And I'm not putting that Christian music down, I loved the CCM I grew up with, but sometimes I wonder if we were inadvertently lied to.

DW: Oh, absolutely. It's terrible theology and it's pretty racist too. They started off blaming rock & roll and tracing it back to the Africans and their voodoo music. Rock & roll dancing supposedly led to sex and it was pretty pathetic theology overall, really. They would've been better to try and teach us about what's redeemable in culture and what isn't, and given people some framework to make their own choices based on those kinds of things, as opposed to dictating what's on the naughty list.

It was quite arrogant too, to suggest that only Christians had the truth and could write music with any weight to it. As you grow up you become well aware of the truth statements of many people who wouldn't consider themselves Christians, you know?

BW: There's plenty of non-Christians making great art that is not evil.

DW: Absolutely. If we're all made in God's image, then God will inspire anyone.

Dave White (The Revs)

BW: I kind of feel like I missed out on a lot of good music growing up. While I've certainly made up for it since, I don't believe it has had a negative influence on my relationship with God. But then I think, well maybe that wasn't so bad, especially as a teenager, to be sheltered a little bit from that.

DW: Yep. I think if my life-journey hadn't intersected with YFC at that pivotal age then things may have turned out different for me. There were some other churches that were a whole lot more conservative. You couldn't dance and if you did then you were holding the devil's hand.

There was some other pretty severe stuff that I remember about other peers of mine, who'd tried to play some rock & roll that inspired dancing. And most of those guys have walked away from the faith, so... you know? It's understandable, in a sense, because they were treated so appallingly by the congregation or elders or key people in leadership.

It's just crazy, crazy stuff. I remember a certain leader who didn't want the Revs to play at a Christian youth camp. He told the boss of the camp to take us off the list because we were obviously anti-Christ in the way we dressed and performed. So we did suffer a little bit, but at the same time YFC supported us and backed us. We didn't personally face any persecution. Scepticism, yes.

BW: You were dressed as Reverends with dog collars and everything?

DW: That's correct, Brett.

BW: Some thought it was blasphemous?

Let's Back Up a Bit

THE REVS. FROM LEFT: MARTY WHITE, DAVE WHITE, AARON WHEELER, STEVE IRVINE.

DW: Yeah. There were some who thought we were taking the piss. But it was meant to be based on those costume bands of the 1960s, I suppose. Well-dressed suits kind of guys. I don't know. I can't remember the exact inspiration.

BW: It was a good gimmick.

DW: Well, you know, people were a bit confused as to where we were coming from with our choice of music.

BW: Well, I didn't realise that the 'Revs' was short for the 'Reverends' until I saw the outfits. How did the band start?

Dave White (The Revs)

DW: We were just a bunch of mates. We basically knew each other in youth group. There was the Capital Teen Convention (CTC) after the school holidays.

CTC was a major talent competition run by YFC where local youth groups and YFC centres would gather at the Michael Fowler Centre in Wellington and compete in several different categories over a weekend.

My mother actually said, 'You should go and sing at CTC.' So that's what we did. We put one song together, '[Gotta] Serve Somebody' by Bob Dylan, and took the bus down to Wellington and performed our song in Revs outfits. The bass player went to the chorus halfway through the second verse, so that was awkward for me ... but, ah, these things happen! So we actually won that year, The Most... oh, what do you call it? Most Potential Band or something.

BW: Most Promising.

DW: Most Promising! So that was huge! And, you know, for me, being onstage was like a release. I was an introvert who suddenly felt at home onstage. I could be an exhibitionist, you know? It was great!

BW: How long ago was this?

DW: 1983? '84? I was about 15 or 16. We practised and rehearsed like you would not believe. The YFC office gave us the key to a space that we used as a practice room. So that became our hobby really. We used to play for hours and hours. We just loved it.

Let's Back Up a Bit

BW: Was there a particular leader of the band?

DW: Oh, that would be me.

BW: Are you happy for that to go on record?

DW: Yeah. I think it's unequivocal. [Laughter] Ah, yeah, I mostly chose the songs and mostly organised stuff. Then my brother [Marty] joined the band, so there was Fleetwood Mac type tension there. [Laughter]

I suggest Gallagher brothers (from Oasis) type tension might be more appropriate.

BW: So Marty was a later addition?

DW: Yeah, I realised I wasn't that flash a singer and Marty was quite a good singer. Well, *better* anyway. So he sung most of the songs and I took on less vocals. So that worked alright, and he was more of a frontman, and so we became a four-piece. He played a bit of keys, a bit of Korg poly-something-or-rather.

BW: Was there any sort of mission for the band or was it all just for fun?

DW: Oh, nah, nah. Well, I speak for myself but, yeah, nah, there was definitely a feeling of evangelism as a fervent young Christian. I always remember Glenn Kaiser [Rez Band] saying, 'The world doesn't need another covers band.' So that kind of stuck with me. So for us, the music was a vehicle to try and share Jesus.

So playing the pubs was an opportunity to share the Gospel in song-matic form. So I was quite harsh on … you know … we

Dave White (The Revs)

weren't allowed to swear and drink in public and all that kind of stuff. We were trying to be honest. We prayed before shows.

BW: Did you?!

DW: Oh, yeah! We had our little Madonna huddle. [Laughter]

BW: Wow. Sorry to sound so surprised by that. I've been in enough music projects with you in the past to know that this no longer happens. Not a criticism, but I wonder what has happened over time for that sort of thing to cease to exist?

DW: Yeah, I'm offended you wouldn't think we would pray. We were wearing Reverend dog collars. [Laughter]

It's probably just the usual spiritual pilgrimage from earnest to jaded. But I think, more earnestly, it's actually symptomatic of a quieter robust faith. Having the knowledge that music breathes sacred because the Creator fashioned it so. It doesn't become sacred and blessed because we pray feeble prayers. Nothing wrong with praying though; I'm sure less jaded Christians are doing it.

BW: There's very little of the Revs' music out there; it's all buried in the depths of your garage. I was quite young when you were in full swing, but I did see you play a few times. But remind me as to what a classic Revs' set list would look like. I remember a song that I thought was called 'Lucy and Ramona' but I found out the other day, it is actually called 'Cruisin'.

DW: Yeah, that is correct. Michael Nesmith.

BW: Why would you cover that song?

Let's Back Up a Bit

DW: Yeah. That's quite insane.

BW: And how does that fit in with sharing Jesus?

DW: It was an inherent number. I remember just writing the lyrics out to that song. It just captured me at intermediate school. We weren't that religious that we couldn't slip the odd song in that had no Gospel reference whatsoever, and that was one of our crowd favourites. A typical gig would have had three or four [Bob] Dylan *Slow Train Coming* songs or anything off his gospel albums.

We had 'Shot of Love', 'Covenant Woman', just about all of them got an airing at some point. 'Slow Train Coming', 'When You Gonna Wake Up', 'Serve Somebody' had about ten different versions through the years. So it was a heavy weighting on the Dylan gospel songs. And then we did a Steve Taylor song once, 'This Disco (Used to Be a Cute Cathedral)'. That was early days. There was a Devo song.

BW: More devil's music.

DW: Yeah, yeah, yeah. We didn't write our own songs; we just twisted other people's songs. We did a John Hiatt number. We did 'Faith' by Violent Femmes. We were really into Violent Femmes.

BW: 'Sign o' the Times' by Prince.

DW: Yes. We sure did. That was a good one. We did 'New Year's Day' by U2. We did quite a bit of U2. But vocally we were absolute rubbish, so that kind of ended up in Devo style as well.

Dave White (The Revs)

BW: So in doing all of these covers, one would think that Glenn Kaiser's comment about the world not needing another covers band didn't stick with you at all!

DW: Ha! Well, if we could write songs we would have. We just weren't songwriters, but we were great song destructors. I guess what Glenn's line meant to me was, 'Why add another band playing 'Sweet Home Alabama' and 'April Sun in Cuba' to the scene?' There was a sense, as earnest Christians, that our choice of songs was going to be different from the status quo... and not Status Quo covers.

BW: Pun intended! Fair enough. So at the same time, I guess you're listing your influences. Bob Dylan, Devo... But musically, the Revs didn't sound like Bob Dylan.

DW: No. Well, we were just learning to play really.

BW: But you had a lot of energy.

DW: Yeah, yeah. We had a fantastic drummer. Why we were reasonably successful was really the foundation of Aaron Wheeler's drumming. My guitaring was okay. We kind of worked well together; his hi-hat and my rhythm. The bass [Steve Irvine] was good. It served the song.

Perhaps in typical Kiwi fashion, Dave not only undersells the capabilities of the band as a strong musical unit but also the role of his brother as frontman.

BW: What about your brother? For many punters Marty would have been the face of the band, as lead singers tend to be. And while, at times, he may have been a little self-conscious as a vocalist, he also carried a certain swagger.

If you were Keith Richards, Marty was certainly Mick Jagger but, in my opinion, he was more like Anthony Kiedis before the world at large knew who the Red Hot Chili Peppers were. If those singers lack anything as vocalists, they make up for it as front men.

DW: [Laughter] Yeah, we had some brutal arguments, me and Marty. We have very different musical tastes and tastes in general. But yes, he had some balls. We played support for the Exponents at Waikato University for Orientation one year.

We played a 40-minute set under full hall fluoro lighting. We played 20 minutes too long and were getting punished by an unimpressed crowd. But Marty had the demeanour to abuse the audience for not being into us… without the cover of darkness. [Laughter]

That's a great memory. But he did have the confidence to be the frontman for sure. At our reunion gig, with more maturity, I could see he was pretty good at his shtick.

Parachute Festival celebrated its 20th anniversary in 2010 and invited a whole bunch of artists of yesteryear to perform, the Revs included.

BW: There was a certain sense of swagger to the whole band as if you all agreed that style was just as important as the music. That the way in which one carries themselves onstage (perhaps offstage too) is a vital ingredient for a successful rock band, even a Christian one. This was tangible onstage, but one example seen offstage if I may…

DW: Sure. This should be good! Ha!

Dave White (The Revs)

BW: As an impressionable young teen, I attended the inaugural Christian music festival, Shelterbelt, in 1989 and you guys made your entrance through the campground in an old stylish black car; it might've been an old Falcon. But to me it was like the parting of the Red Sea, as if to say, 'Step aside everyone. The Revs have arrived.' Was any of that *coolness* cultivated at all?

DW: I had a black '63 Mercedes 190. Then a Falcon XP wagon. The Merc was brilliant. You could pretty much put our gear plus the P.A. in the boot. But nothing and everything was cultivated about us. We just liked what we liked and acted as naturally as we could while we spent an hour in the mirror preening. Usual teenage angst. But yeah, if I had a dollar for everyone that ever said to me, 'You guys are way too cool.' Personally, I was shy and that got translated by others, usually, as me being cool fulla aloof styles.

BW: Either way, it all added to the group's success and popularity, I think. As well as well-performed music. What did that success look like at the time?

DW: Well, we were flown all around the country playing all kinds of youth group events. And youth groups would write fan mail. So we'd play just about every weekend at some youth group and we played a lot in Auckland with Hoi Polloi and that scene with all the Auckland bands.

And through YFC there were a lot of connections as well. Youth rally type work. So because it was kind of a new thing and people felt there was an emerging sense of freedom that it was okay to play rock & roll, then everyone wanted a piece of it and we just came along as a band at the right time.

The whole scene had its own fanzine, *SPAMM* magazine,

which was highly critical to its success. They would do some great interviews and, based on our Mainstage Festival performance, we made the cover of *SPAMM* magazine, which was out of control. It was instant fandom. Yeah, the dressing up as Revs thing, the energy, the fact that most of the songs had some kind of blatant Christian message, the Dylan songs, all meant that we got the tick by most youth pastors for us to come on down.

BW: Wow.

DW: Yeah, no one knew about our coke habits at that point, so it was all good. [Laughter – just a joke, dear readers]

BW: Did you ever get a sense that this success could reach across into mainstream circles?

DW: Well, maybe to a certain extent with more people coming to our shows. But the main inhibitor to all of that was we were never writing our own material, so we always knew that we were not going to ever be anything serious, and we never grew into the songwriting role.

But there was a high level of originality and creativity to our shows in terms of the music. Sometimes you couldn't even connect the original version of some songs to what we came out with. Like 'Sign o' the Times' for instance. There was a fairly dramatic arrangement of that. So yeah, there was a lot of creativity and originality in our shows but not from a songwriting or lyrical perspective. We just loved the idea of twisting other people's ideas.

BW: And you've done that ever since.

Dave White (The Revs)

MARTY WHITE GRACES THE COVER OF THE AUGUST 1987 ISSUE OF SPAMM.

Let's Back Up a Bit

DW: Yeah, that's a trademark. Back in those days there were always quite a lot of band competitions in pubs. So we would always enter those and always reach the finals. That was quite rewarding to know that we could mix it up with the heavies in the local music scene.

BW: It's very hard to go and dial up your music online. How would you describe the Revs' sound to the readers?

DW: Um... yeah, it was kind of bluesy, funky... There were moments of Stevie Ray Vaughan kind of thing... [long pause] Oh, I don't know...

This is not a good description of the Revs' sound.

BW: I know it's a hard question for any artist, really, but you were quite different stylistically, would you agree?

DW: Yeah, well we weren't very proficient players, so we just made our style up. You know what I mean? We could never rip the songs off like they were supposed to sound anyway, we didn't have the talent to do that, or the *will* to do that, so we just did our own thing. So yeah, it was a fairly unique sound.

BW: Those Bob Dylan gospel songs are overtly Christian, which is something I see less of these days from Christian artists. Of course, it will always exist. I mean if you listen to Life FM for long enough, you're going to hear it, but it seemed like *every* Christian musician had overt Christian lyrics a while ago. If you do these days, then you might be regarded as a worship artist.

DW: Yeah, I couldn't really comment on what's going on in the current Christian scene, I don't have enough reference points. But if you're right, then in some ways I'm relieved that people aren't writing Christian lyrics because the stuff was so corny and cheesy.

You know, Bob Dylan had three to six months of a Christian Bible course and then he delivered that album [*Slow Train Coming*] which smashed all the CCM guys out of the water in terms of content. So... you know... just saying. Part of me is relieved that people aren't trying as much. But that would be the same with evangelism in general, you know? It's out of favour to some degree.

BW: Speaking of evangelism, how did you get involved in YFC?

DW: Well, as a kid, it would be a big night out if I could go to the Certain Sounds show. I have early memories of going to those kinds of shows. The Founders Theatre, sometimes at Claudelands Showgrounds and also there were some outdoor shows at the Waikato Stadium [then known as Rugby Park].

BW: Yeah, I remember going to one or two at Rugby Park. Thousands of people would be there! I remember getting turned away once at the Founders Theatre. Couldn't get in!

DW: Yeah, they were hugely popular. A big deal. And friends of mine were going to the local YFC youth night, which was Campus Life, so I got mildly involved in that. And I also went to the local rallies at the Founders, which were monthly multi-media shows. So because we played at CTC in Wellington, and then became involved in the local scene, we ended up playing at their shows. Like I say, they were very encouraging and supportive.

Let's Back Up a Bit

BW: And you eventually started working for YFC.

DW: Yeah. Three or four months later I made a decision to serve Jesus. They used to have mission-based shows on Sunday afternoons, and I made a response there, which was a significant turning point in terms of my life choice, at that age. I would've been 18 or 19. And through that I quit the rock stardom of the Revs, which was on the cusp of breaking through, and spent a year on the road with Certain Sounds 1988. So that was an interesting experience.

BW: How did the boys in the band take that?

DW: Ah, they weren't impressed to be honest.

BW: Did the Revs carry on after your stint on Certain Sounds '88?

DW: Yeah, we went for a couple of years after that. I can't remember the reasons for our demise. Steve and I formed another band with some musos from New Plymouth; Scotty Pearson, a great drummer later of Elemeno P fame, and a great singer, Tereora Crane (Marcus Crane, as he was known in those days). We started a band called the Jordans. A new venture where we were going to write new music. We put out a little EP which is now lost to the world, aside from Tereora's 4-Track copy.

BW: I remember a Revs' gig at Riverlea Theatre, Hamilton. Bob Dylan's 50th birthday celebration, which would have been in 1991. That wasn't the Revs' last gig was it?

DW: No. I think we had several last gigs!

Dave White (The Revs)

BW: I'm pretty sure it was [Hamilton band] the Pilgrims' first gig ever that same night and it was like a handing down of the baton. The Revs passing it on to the Pilgrims, who came across as a mini-Revs to some who witnessed it. Similar sort of sound.

The guitarist for the Pilgrims, Karl Berzins, designed the artwork for the cover of this book.

DW: Oh yeah! Wasn't it just?! After we split, we got the call up for the opening support slot for Stryper when they came, and we couldn't do it. That would've been an experience. [Laughter – especially considering Dave's hatred towards that sort of music]

At that time, the Minister of Internal Affairs was on national news trying to stop Stryper from entering the country because they dressed in drag [they wore spandex outfits and heavy make-up, as did most hair-metal bands of the 1980s] and were obviously un-Christian even though they claimed to be Christian [sarcasm noted].

The Minister of Internal Affairs trying to stop Stryper! I mean there were other things going on in the world that he could've put his attention to, but there you go. What they were producing was poisoning the minds of New Zealanders [more sarcasm].

BW: Well, as funny as it sounds now, I can relate to that as people told me off for wearing a Stryper T-shirt to church. Which is ridiculous.

DW: It's ridiculous now, but at the time it was serious stuff. There was another Hamilton band that played a New Year's Eve show up the country somewhere, and they got a five-page letter from somebody there who witnessed people dancing and they had all of these Scriptures about how evil that was and how dare they inspire people to have a good time. Another friend of mine was called in to some elders' meeting because they had been dancing the pogo, which is apparently an upright masturbation dance. [Incredulous laughter]

Funny times. But that was the craziness of the cultural milieu at the time.

BW: Yeah, it's obvious that the rock & roll detractors didn't like the music – which is fine – but instead of saying, 'Look, I just really don't like the music,' they would say, 'Here's some Scriptures to suggest that the music is evil.' Would you agree with that?

DW: That's a pretty fair assessment. I think there was a whole lot of people who just didn't like the music and therefore it kind of connects well with some secondary theological reasoning why it was dangerous to participate in.

But again, it was a theology that allowed you to exclude yourself from the world, you know? Not engage in it. So it was really an isolation of a righteous movement. And some of them probably had good intentions and were trying to care for the young people but were obviously misguided.

BW: And you also had influential ministers and leaders. I mean, for me, it was Jimmy Swaggart. He was huge in our house.

DW: Right. Was he anti-rock?

BW: Oh yeah, he wrote a book on it. But he's a musician. His cousin is the famous rock & roller, Jerry Lee Lewis.

Dave White (The Revs)

DRY HAIR IS A SECRET INGREDIENT FOR ANY SUCCESSFUL BAND.
FROM LEFT: STEVE IRVINE, AARON WHEELER, MARTY WHITE, DAVE WHITE.

DW: No way!

BW: Jimmy plays piano just like him really. He tears it up on piano. It's that 1950s rock & roll style of piano playing. And Jimmy has released dozens of albums and sold millions.

And I think to myself, if you're going to say that a type of music is evil, where do draw the line, Jimmy? You're playing Southern Gospel or whatever you want to call it, but when you play a solo, there's no difference between you and your cousin who played rock & roll, the so-called devil's music.

DW: That's epic. Somehow, I ended up at a Bill Gothard conference up in Auckland and he was super anti-rock & roll. But they had this shredding violin player. If you'd changed that to electric guitar it would have changed the whole context, but because it was a violin, he got away with it.

There was a standing ovation when he was shredding away, and me and my mates were just sitting there thinking, 'This is weird.' The sacred versus the secular is a horrible divide and you and I have spent our lives trying to disengage from that.

BW: Well, I embraced it in the '80s...

DW: Oh, yeah, same. That's the lens in which we look through life and we were taught and encouraged to do that. But it's not a Jewish way of looking at the world, you know? God's in all the world and He's not just limited to the Christian playground. So again, it leads to the kind of viewpoints those leaders have. Because their theology is so narrow, their viewpoints become narrow.

BW: Let's get back to YFC and how you started working for them.

DW: Oh, yeah! So I did the tour of New Zealand with Certain Sounds '88 and visited lots of YFC centres around the country. At that time YFC was very popular and did lots of significant work with young people, and so I saw what they were doing and how they did it and that looked appealing to me.

So I went back to Hamilton and offered my services to YFC Waikato under Gus Row, the boss man. So I did a seven-year stint there where I was basically hired to work with musicians and artists and create multi-media presentations of the Gospel. I was in charge of youth rallies and camps, but I was a part of everything to some degree, but they would've been my main responsibilities.

BW: What would a typical week look like for you?

DW: Well, you know we turned around some of those rallies every month so, when I look back at the workload, it was pretty severe. To pull together an hour-and-a-half show every month was quite full-on really. I would manage a group of people who were committed to putting these things on, so you'd design a show around a theme and away you'd go. You'd work with young people, new vocalists, put some bands together, so it was a great breeding ground for musicians to try their stuff out.

YFC was great because it was a platform where lots of young people from different churches could meet. It was interdenominational, which was its strength. There were lots of creative people around; people like Brett Major and Darryl Parsons who have gone on to work for creative agencies.

So my job was to work on songs and do some slideshows, some visual stuff, some dramas and, along with other people, put the show together. Pack-ins and pack-outs are a strong memory. Rolling cables. But a lot of good times too. And the Hamilton rallies were very indicative of what other YFC centres did around the country too.

BW: Well, I would just hang out for those rallies as a young guy. They were a huge event on the calendar. The youth group used to go to the Founders Theatre and be treated to all these bands. I used to enjoy watching a young Bruce Parker on drums. I think he was about 14 but playing like a skilled 40-year-old. It was a great platform for up-and-coming musicians.

Let's Back Up a Bit

DW: Yeah, unbelievable. And also, we were treated to some Auckland artists like Derek Lind and Dallas Graham. Charisma from Palmerston North. So all these other bands would have a platform to come and play.

BW: You just don't see that kind of thing now. I mean there was Parachute Festival and now Festival One, and you might get played on Life FM, but you didn't have Life FM back then. That's quite different to what you and other YFC centres around the country were doing.

DW: Yeah, it was a pretty unique platform for musicians to develop their craft, that's for sure. But the churches provide those platforms these days, to some degree.

BW: Any particular memories from the YFC days where you stop and think, 'Flip, that was worth it'? You did so many events but is there one thing that stands out?

DW: Ah, we wrote an hour and a half show that involved characters, called *Lust Never Sleeps*. In terms of a creative thing, it was pretty impressive that we could pull that off with just a bunch of young, creative writers. And that show toured a bit. We took a bus down to Taumaranui. That was pretty cool to think that we could *tour* a *show*, you know? There was a lot of fun with that.

I still know a girl that I had a conversation with who made steps to follow Jesus, and still is today. So that's one notch stuck on the belt of brilliance. But a lot of that stuff you never hear back from. And YFC wasn't a healthy experience for everybody. Some would say it exploited their talent. Not everyone has a healthy remembrance, especially some people from the touring teams, Y-ONE and Certain Sounds. There was a lot of expectation but perhaps we could've done more to support their faith as opposed to their talent.

BW: After you and I toured in Certain Sounds '94, you were involved in training other teams leading up to the end of Certain Sounds altogether [the late '90s]. Did you get a sense that maybe it wasn't working anymore?

DW: Oh yeah. Definitely. When I toured in '88, we played at the Avondale Racecourse to, I think I'm right in saying, 15,000 people. When I toured with you in '94, a good attendance would've been around 800-1,000 people. That's a significant drop.

Over that six-year period there was a huge shift in culture. Certain Sounds was based on taking Top 40 radio songs with some kind of merit, basically a glorified covers band with stories of life in Jesus by the musicians on the tour, wrapped up with a sermon and an appeal at the end and that was it. And that seemed to attract busloads of people in '88.

Bus after bus of high schoolers who had seen a snippet of the show at their lunch-time concert or during their assembly, came along to the evening show to hear more.

But then you started to get sub-genres of music that people didn't like. Radio stations started to proliferate. Little River Band's number one hit once appealed to 90 percent of the market. Years later, similar songs only attracted very little because sub-genres like heavy metal, hip-hop, punk, were now popular.

So putting a band together that would appeal to a large audience became less and less doable. It was not a winning premise. And obviously the cost of putting a band on the road for a year was exorbitant. So at the end of the day, YFC said, 'Well, bang for buck, it's not looking flash.'

Let's Back Up a Bit

BW: Right. So the demise of the touring teams was due to more and more genres emerging?

DW: That's what I'm saying.

BW: Wow. I've never thought about that before. The range of repertoire in 1994 – Metallica songs alongside Madonna songs – wouldn't have been so broad in 1988.

DW: Yeah. And culture got a little savvier too. There was more discernment of authenticity. So a guy getting up there playing a cover of a pop song wasn't treated as authentic by the culture. That would be another point to its demise.

But great nostalgia! I mean, wow. It was great for its time; put a bunch of people on the road. It was pretty radical. The first tour was in a couple of Holden station wagons and it had a drum-kit, so it was pretty 'out there'.

BW: YFC kind of morphed into this thing called Incedo.

DW: Yeah. It wasn't just a name change; it was a complete transformation.

BW: What does Incedo mean?

DW: It's Latin for 'going forward'.

BW: Let's talk about how it went forward.

DW: Well, Gus Row would give you better info on that as he was one of the head honchos.

Dave White (The Revs)

BW: Sure. But this is about you.

DW: Oh, yeah, yeah, yeah! YFC was a prescriptive, top-down, American-based operation. So you had things like a Rock Solid club for intermediate aged kids and Campus Life for high schoolers. We also had Te Ora Hou for at-risk young people.

These groups would work independently on a weekly small-group model and then come together at a rally for an appeal, and the discipleship would go on to a church, because we weren't a church. We were called a para-church. So that ended.

Some of the YFC leaders at the time were unconvinced that the YFC model was working in the culture of the time. That must've been the late-'90s, early 2000s. So some of them presented a new model to go forward and some of the YFC centres bought into it and some of them didn't.

So it wasn't a tension-free change. For those who moved on it became a faith community, so we owned a lot more of our own spiritual formation. That was part of the motivation. There were lots of differences, but the main thing was there was a set of values and a set of practices that would denote being an Incedo member. So membership became a thing.

If you became an Incedo member then you would commit to the values and practices of Incedo. That gave us a lot of freedom and permission to try new things because, instead of doing Campus Life clubs, you could do anything you like as long as those values were adhered to.

So a lot of cool stuff has happened over the years. But in terms of numbers, it's shrunk a lot since YFC. We're looking at a small but committed group. It's a nationwide community, so there are members throughout the country.

BW: And what is your particular role?

Let's Back Up a Bit

DW: My role in Incedo in Hamilton has been to be part of the faith community. We meet every two weeks for spiritual formation. And outside of that I've curated some large art events; one celebrates Easter (Stations of the Cross) and one celebrates Christmas (Trees at the Meteor).

There are also service projects in Te Araroa that I help facilitate and other projects as they come and go throughout the year. But Incedo has made some positive bridge-building towards the queer community. I would say that's a pretty cool trademark of Incedo currently.

BW: Yeah, that's pretty radical.

DW: Well, it shouldn't be, but it perhaps is. Yeah, the church in general has not been helpful in engaging the queer community; lots of judgement and bad calls that have hurt a lot people.

BW: Well... [long pause] If only I was smart enough to carry that conversation on! [Laughter]

In terms of discussing it in this book though – and I'm trying to be careful how I say this – that whole thing is reminiscent of how more and more Christians have changed their view towards rock music over time. But I'm certainly not putting music and homosexuality alongside one another as if they're the same thing.

The Bible seems to be more outspoken about homosexuality than it is about the dangers of music. But it seems to me that some Christians' views towards the queer community are changing, or at least being challenged, and you are an example of that. I think I could say quite confidently that your view would've been quite different 30 years ago to what it is now.

DW: Yes.

Dave White (The Revs)

BW: What was the catalyst for that change in view?

DW: I think it was a slow progression. I think for me, being married to a Māori woman, showed me what it's like to be part of a minority culture and to be exposed to values that I was unaware of and to be challenged about my sub-racist prejudices. So I think that was probably the underlining motivation.

You suddenly become aware of the viewpoints you might have held, which actually have no weight in reality. And I guess just reading people's commentaries such as Tony Campolo, Brian McLaren, and some of those kinds of voices that are sympathetic and compassionate towards the queer community. They would've had some kind of influence on me.

Plus, my personal belief in a God of overall generosity and goodness to people and some deeper reflection on those Bible verses that some people use to keep people out and how the verses, perhaps, aren't the barriers that people think they are.

They were written in a certain context about a certain thing. We're talking about male and male sexual relations based around sex in the temple kind of thing. Well, that's quite different to same-sex orientated people in a committed relationship. So you've got to be talking apples and apples and oranges and oranges.

BW: Well, I'm not sure that a shift in people's views all of a sudden makes those views 'right'. It might just mean that more people are now accepting the wrong thing! And therefore, maybe listening to rock music *is* evil after all this time, *especially* the Christian stuff! [Laughter]

Seriously though, what I think you *are* right about is that Christians should demonstrate love to *everybody* despite our viewpoints; that is what Jesus did and still does. That is to say, I think He extends grace to those who genuinely turn away from sin. Those who stubbornly do not, are not gracefully excused.

But that gives me no excuse to be totally arrogant and hard-hearted to those who don't. I don't think that is Christ-like. And that reminds me of a group email you sent out; one of your infamous 'rants' about your trip to the Sydney Mardi Gras, and included in the rant was a photo of you standing there holding a sign simply saying, 'Sorry.' You were apologising to the queer community on behalf of the Christian community who, as you suggest, had not shown grace and compassion. I was moved by that.

DW: Yes, well you see that may never have happened underneath the YFC umbrella because there wouldn't have been that same kind of freedom for the members. And probably not everyone in Incedo agreed with it, but that's the beauty of Incedo and the faith community; that we can hold tension. There's no dictatorship from up top. And that was truly an awesome experience. People were moved to tears at the Mardi Gras as they saw our signs.

BW: How do you balance all of this between what certain leaders say and what the Bible might say about it?

DW: Well, I think you knocked it on the head there because it's all about how you interpret the Bible. If you interpret it a certain way, then you're going to come out with a certain view. So you can argue those four verses till the cows come home... and I think there's a continuum of belief; some people are affirming of homosexuality and they're open and inclusive, and others are less affirming. And that's fair.

Everyone's got their own perspective on it. They've got their own understanding of the Bible and their own understanding of sexuality issues and orientation. But above all, love is the mantra of Christ. So there isn't any excuse to hold these beliefs without love.

Dave is married with three children. Since this interview, he left Incedo and started up a café in the main street of Hamilton called Yalla Yalla. More recently, he has returned to high school teaching. So I guess that means more Santa outfits and chainsaws!

Derek Lind (photo credit: Belinda Bradley).

DEREK LIND

I was exposed to Derek Lind's music as a teenager, sometime during the 1980s, and while his social-conscience lyrics were a bit grown-up for me at the time, I appreciated the fact that he seemed to have something important to say through his music.

In 1991, Dave White invited me to play harmonica for Derek at a YFC rally at the Founders Theatre. A major gig for someone fresh out of high school. I remember hanging out with Derek in the 'green room' before we went on stage and I was impressed by this 'superstar' of Kiwi music going out of his way to chat to this young 'nobody'.

I always enjoyed Derek's blues sensibilities and found his live gigs entertaining, including the witty and thought-provoking banter in between songs. Looking at it now, with a bit more maturity and musical experience, it's not difficult to appreciate the skill and craft that he puts into his songs.

It's also not difficult to understand why he has received critical acclaim for his songwriting throughout his career, which spans four decades. One example: music critic, Graham Reid regards Derek as 'one of the most consistently literate yet most affecting lyricists.'

Fast forward 20 years or so and I find myself in a Bob Dylan tribute band with him. Fast forward later still and I find myself playing in Derek's backing band to promote his absolutely stunning album, *Solo* (2015.)

I caught up with Derek after a rehearsal for an upcoming gig where we chatted about his life and his music.

Brett Wilson: Your songs are a good place to find bits and pieces of your biography so I want to start by mentioning a couple of them. Firstly 'When the Bough Breaks' (*Stations*, 1994):

> My father was a banker / My mother taught piano / I have two brothers; an older and a younger / I was raised in the middle / And I was raised in faith / I was fed and clothed and prayed for / Maybe at night my parents lay awake / And asked, 'Where will the children fall when the bough breaks?' / And we moved from town to town...

Which towns are we talking about?

Derek Lind: Well, my dad was in banking so we moved quite regularly. I was born in Fiji actually. Mum and Dad moved there after they got married and Dad was at the BNZ in Suva, and my older brother and I were both born there.

We came back when I was about three, I think. Lived in Wellington, Levin, Katikati, Dargaville and we came to Auckland when I was about 16. So we moved around a fair bit, which is probably why I'm the traumatised person that I am today. [Laughter]

BW: That song goes on to say:

> And I was given a guitar, but I never really learned to play it / Some things stay exactly as they are.

That's classic Derek Lind self-effacing humour, as you're a fine guitarist. But it sounds like a fairly stable upbringing, not to mention a legacy of faith, when you also consider the song 'My Grandfather' from the same album. It mentions how your grandfather was a preacher.

DL: Well, he wasn't an ordained preacher, he was a lay preacher because we were brought up in the Open Brethren tradition. But both those songs are pretty much on the money in terms of … you know, I haven't made anything up. [Laughter]

BW: Sure. And your grandmother played the organ.

DL: Yeah, he'd preach and she'd pedal. It was an old harmonium.

BW: So no matter where you lived, you always attended an Open Brethren church?

DL: Yep. Pretty much. Because of my dad's financial background he'd often end up in a leadership position or an eldership position, as they have them in the Brethren tradition. But for them personally, as they moved on, they ended up in retirement in Hanmer Springs and became Presbyterian by default, because there wasn't a Brethren church there.

My dad was involved in business and the corporate world so he had a fairly broad vision and understanding of how the world worked, and sometimes in the church community it can be fairly tight and a little bit jaundiced in its thinking.

But Dad had to deal with the secular world in a prominent

way and I always appreciated Dad for that really. He wasn't too dogmatic about certain things and certain behaviour or ways of thinking that define you spiritually.

I mean, I went and studied fine arts at Auckland University, and a lot of other parents in my parents' position would have perhaps objected to that or put up a bit of a fight and suggested I do something a little more vocationally practical, but they were really supportive. And same with the music.

Both Mum and Dad were musicians. Mum was a piano teacher and Dad played a bit of piano and a bit of violin. They lived in small neighbouring towns in the Manawatu and Mum went to my dad's mum for piano lessons in a little town called Shannon, and that's how Mum and Dad met up.

BW: What sort of music did your parents play around the house?

DL: A lot of classical. The closest thing that would have come to contemporary music was a Jim Reeves album called *We Thank Thee*, and I reckon if I heard that album, even to this day, I could probably sing those songs word for word. So there wasn't a lot of contemporary music, but as we got a bit older some of the younger folk in the church would expose us to a few other things and then, of course, I got exposed to [Bob] Dylan and all of that stuff when I was about 14, maybe even a bit younger.

BW: I grew up after the Jesus Movement had given birth to contemporary Christian music. It was frowned upon by many Christians to listen to secular music, and perhaps even Christian rock music. There was a lot of teaching in youth group on the dangers of rock & roll. What did you think of all of that?

DL: Well, I just think it might have caught people by surprise a little bit. To be honest with you, I wasn't ever a great student of the Christian music that was coming out. When I started out, I played secular gigs more than anything. When I was 15 or so I was living in Dargaville and I was singing with the likes of Mark Williams [Top 40 artist and current singer for Dragon] and people like that, and that was when the musical bug sort of hit me.

The first album I ever bought with my own pocket money, when I was probably about 14, would have been the Beatles' *Abbey Road*. The second album I bought was *Bridge Over Troubled Water* by Simon & Garfunkel. The third one was a Bob Dylan album and the fourth one was *After the Gold Rush* by Neil Young. I didn't know anything about half of these people really.

It was quite fortuitous that I chose some good rock role models at the front end. And that shaped my musical direction somewhat. I could just as easily have bought Black Sabbath and Deep Purple albums, you know? That could've taken me in a different direction! [Laughter]

So I wasn't discouraged from having my own independent taste, and I think part of adolescence is it's sort of your job to find stuff that offends your parents to the greatest degree possible. And that's just a natural way to find your own voice and it's a pretty mild form of rebellion, you know what I mean?

BW: Yes, I think it is especially mild today, but I think during that time, the '70s, '80s and even going into the '90s, it was a bigger deal. I don't think my parents were too concerned compared to some others. For some, rock & roll was a no-go zone. Even Christian rock music was an oxymoron: how can something that is 'of the devil' (rock music) be 'of the Lord' at the same time?

DL: Yeah, yeah, yeah. I was subjected to a lot of those sorts of talks at camps and things from people who equated rock music with the primitive jungle drums and it drove people into sexual frenzies and blah-di-blah-di-blah. All of that sort of thing. And there was the ... was it Bob Larson books?

BW: Yeah!

DL: All those sort of anti-rock books and all that sort of thing.

BW: Yes, but wouldn't all of that have come out after you had established yourself as a performer?

DL: Yeah. Well, you gotta understand that when I started out and when I started playing music with Christians, there wasn't such a thing as a Christian music industry.

There was just a scene. I was in a band with some other Christian friends, including the lady that became my wife, and I think there were about four albums out in the Christian bookstores that were palatable to us young people.

There was the *Love Song* album, there might have been some early Larry Norman, maybe Chuck Girard. But, you know, there was just like four, and there were a bunch of Christian bands starting up around town in Auckland here.

And basically what you did was you'd try and be the first person to get hold of one of those albums and claim some of the songs and do a little circuit, you know, the coffee-houses and things. And you sort of had the patent on it, you had the mortgage on that Larry Norman song. So yeah, the industry as such didn't really exist.

BW: This was in the mid-'70s?

DL: Yeah. So it was pretty slim pickings in terms of stuff that was hip to Christian musicians. But the whole Christian music industry started to mushroom a wee bit later and then it became another entity altogether. So we were a wee bit naïve and innocent in those days, you know?

And I think that's what led me to becoming a writer. We could never find enough material to sing in the band because there was such a scarcity of it out there, so I started writing.

The problem was a lot of what I wrote didn't really work in the band context; vocal harmonies and this, that and everything else and so my songs weren't that democratic in terms of finding parts for others to play. So when that band slowly folded or people moved on or got married or whatever, I just kept going on my own and that's how the solo thing happened.

BW: What was your band called?

DL: It was called the Sanctuary Band and it was my wife, Ra, and her older brother – they've both since passed – another mutual friend who owns a chain of music stores around the country, Roger Smith, and his fiancée on bass and vocals, and the drummers were a bit like the Spinal Tap line-up [laughter], they kept coming and going.

But we weren't very good. We were like Dr Hook and the Medicine Show. We were sort of like … we weren't very good … put it that way. But in those days you didn't have to be very good. It was a very forgiving audience, pretty much.

BW: And you'd only play Christian songs?

DL: Yeah. Pretty much. Although if you found a secular song that you thought somehow you could squeeze in there and make it fit, we sometimes did that too because we were starting to question what defines a Christian song. Well I was anyway, and I still don't know the answer to that today!

BW: Yes, it's ambiguous and perhaps it should be. I think God is a lot bigger than our limited definitions, labels and boxes. But music doesn't seem to be as big a deal these days for young people, or youth leaders or pastors, like it was decades ago. I don't think youth groups are playing videos on the evils of Beyoncé or whichever current artist you want to name.

DL: Well, I think I was lucky in that I was brought up to grow a brain that was discerning and to be able to think a little more critically, perhaps. And the things that I studied at school and did well in were the Arts and English. And you have to think a little critically. It's not rote learning or anything like that. You have to think a little more instinctively.

BW: We've just been rehearsing another autobiographical song of yours, 'Somewhere (Just As I Am)' from *12 Good Hours of Daylight* (2002). Perhaps you could fill in a few blanks. It talks about when you were young your family took a trip from a country town...

DL: Dargaville.

BW: To a city stadium...

DL: Western Springs.

BW: To listen to an American preacher...

DL: Billy Graham.

BW: The song suggests that many people responded to an altar call while the choir sang the hymn 'Just As I Am, Without One Plea' and while this had no effect on you at that very moment, something significant seemed to happen to you between that evening and by the time you woke up the next morning.

DL: Well, that's slightly symbolic, but it was sometime later. You see, I grew up in a church tradition where in the morning you had Sunday School and then you had the worship service. And in the Brethren tradition, that was where you took communion and there was no written agenda as such. No formal preaching.

People could stand up. Men. It was very patriarchal. Men could stand up and share a thought, a prayer, a Bible verse, whatever. And at the appointed time someone would pray for the bread and wine and they would be dispensed and end of service.

Then in the evenings they would have a traditional evangelical Gospel service which was pretty hell-fire and brimstone. And for most of my childhood I became a Christian every Sunday night, you know, because I was so petrified in the evening sitting in the car in the dark waiting for Mum and Dad gas-bagging in the church foyer. So I can't think of one particular day, but eventually I felt that I didn't need to pray the sinner's prayer again.

So that song is talking about the transition interphase, rather than just some sort of bolt out of the blue experience. But the Billy Graham experience is one of those benchmark moments in your life. It was a big deal. There was a lot of coverage of him at the time on national TV. Nowadays it mightn't get a paragraph in a national newspaper. But I guess at the time, New Zealand was a much smaller place and it was very newsworthy.

Let's Back Up a Bit

BW: 'Somewhere (Just As I Am)' also name-checks a few musical influences:

> When I was young / in '69 I was 14 years old / And my head was filled with music / Hendrix and *Abbey Road* and Sly and the Family Stone.

DL: Well, that was in the Dargaville years when I'd hang out with Mark Williams. He and I were buddies for a year or two. I used to hang out with him and he exposed me to a lot of stuff. He was a year or two older than me.

BW: So what sort of Christian music had an impact on you at the time?

DL: Andraé Crouch. The first time I saw him in concert and also Larry Norman. The first time I saw him in concert too. I would say Larry Norman most of all because I could see myself emulating him more than I could see myself emulating Andraé Crouch's band, you know? I wasn't soulful enough to do that. I was just a little white kid. 'Larry Norman,' I thought, 'yeah just one man and his guitar.' I thought that could work.

There were a few English bands that I quite liked; Malcolm & Alwyn, Fool's Wisdom. Those guys. But I never really got into anything that was too nice. I liked the edginess of … because at the time I was into Dylan and that too. I was getting into blues music and stuff that was a bit more edgy. It wasn't radical in terms of dressing up in high heels and spitting fire type edgy, you know? It just had a grittiness and an earthiness and an honesty that struck a chord with me.

BW: Randy Stonehill? He's a man-and-his-guitar kind of artist.

DL: Yeah, not so much. I'm not sure why. I never really followed him that much. I think Guy [Wishart] and I opened for him. It was years ago. Him and Phil Keaggy at the [Auckland] Town Hall. I remember learning some Randy Stonehill songs. I was probably listening to a lot more secular music of that ilk than I was Christian music at the time. I mean, I always have to be honest.

BW: I've always thought that there are a few similarities between you and Larry Norman, even the timbre of your voice. But then I guess both of you were inspired by Neil Young?

DL: Yeah, well that's the thing. You share common reference points don't you?

BW: Yeah. Was there a particular Larry Norman album that you really got into?

DL: Ah, what was the one where he got into trouble for being a bit naked on the cover?

BW: [Laughter] *So Long Ago, The Garden.*

DL: Yeah, that one. I really liked that one actually.

The album cover features a lion in a field superimposed over Norman. This apparently caused some people to believe he was exposing pubic hair.

DL: And of course, I was into the Beatles and the [Rolling] Stones. And even then, because I was developing my own writing and it was veering more towards a solo thing rather than a

Let's Back Up a Bit

group thing, I was tending to look at solo singers and to listen to singer/songwriters more I suppose.

There was James Taylor, Carole King, Crosby Stills & Nash. I wasn't that interested in anything too heavy metal-ish. I wasn't into the whole art-rock thing of Yes or Emerson Lake & Palmer. I *tried* to like it, because it was quite hip. [Laughter]

BW: Another autobiographical song from 12 *Good Hours of Daylight* (2002) is 'A Bad Song Everyday' which opens with:

> When I was younger / I used to, pretty much, write a bad song every day.

As self-effacing as that sounds…

DL: No, that's actually the truth! [Laughter]

BW: But that's actually the approach taken by some of the greatest songwriters in the world and, while they appear to churn out nothing but greatness, it's somewhat comforting to know they have probably written a lot of bad songs that never saw the light of day. Like the professional songwriting educator, Pat Pattison, says, 'Don't be afraid to write crap; because crap makes great fertiliser.'

DL: Well, people say, 'How do I become a songwriter?' And I say, 'Well, you just gotta write songs. And the first 50 or 100 songs you write probably won't be worthy of singing to the family pet.' But you gotta do that stuff and eventually you start to hit pay dirt. Well, figuratively. [Laughter]

I think the first songs you usually write are sort of full of teenage angst. It's you against the world and, you know, the hard road you have to walk and here you are, you're 15 and you've hardly left the bedroom, you know? But they're very self-indulgent sort of things and, if you're a Christian, you felt a pressure to make every song have a happy ending spiritually. That was the expectation.

BW: You felt the pressure to do that?

DL: Yeah, well it might have been self-imposed, but you're sort of thinking that this song could save somebody. So it became a tract with melody attached to it. [Laughter]
    It was like Russian propaganda paintings, you know? Obvious as all get-go. It takes a while to realise that, like many of the Psalms, not everything has to be rounded out. I think there should be a sense of hope that comes out of the music that you make.
    It may not come out in every song but if you look over the body of work you can say, well, there was light at the end of the tunnel or something. But not every song has to end with, 'Become a Christian and you can be like me.' [Laughter]

BW: Well, it's a bit like life. Sometimes there just doesn't seem to be any answer and you do feel helpless.

DL: Yeah. And that's alright. But whether you need to subject the global population to that song or to that sentiment is another thing. If you're just putting out a bunch of cathartic wailing and gnashing of teeth to music, it might be good for you and you might get it off your chest, but I don't know whether there's any great need to release it to an unsuspecting public or not.
    So if you are going to be talking about these sorts of things you have to talk about them in such a way that it becomes relatable. There's some sense of commonality. Even if it's quite

deeply personal things or events, there has to be something in it for the listener.

But then you've got to care enough about your listener and not … I mean that's essentially the main beef I started to have with Christian music: the songs didn't give enough credit to the listener to fill in the gaps. So we'd spell it out to them because we were so desperately scared that our songs would be misinterpreted.

You see, good art is open to interpretation. What you see can be a bit different to what I see. The problem with Christians is that they're scared of it being misinterpreted or taken the wrong way in case people miss the punchline or the message. Now that's not a pressure a secular musician feels at all. But we have this other agenda that we have to sort of impose or superimpose on top of the song, and I'm not too sure whether that's correct. Do you know what I mean?

BW: Well, I think maybe that's changed a little bit over time for some Christian music, to give it some credit. But not too long ago music seemed to be the art form where the expectation from a lot of Christians was, 'Oh, you're a Christian? And a musician? Well you better have a sermon in your song.'

Whereas other art forms … I could be wrong, but you're a visual artist as well as a musician, so was there the same pressure to paint the cross in every painting you did?

DL: Well, I think part of the thing is that music has been very much a part of the church, right through. I mean the church has been the nursery for great music. A lot of the great black soul and R&B music came out of the church. These people paid their dues in the church.

And so music's always been deemed more *useful* in the church than some other art forms and because there's more familiarity with music, music and the church going hand in hand, or being in partnership as part of the service, there's a greater sensitivity to that art form than there are to others.

Because if you're an artist in the church, they haven't got that much use for you, but music can be quite useful. So yeah, I think there was that expectation that your music had to be used almost as an evangelical platform that perhaps other art forms weren't given that sort of pressure.

A lot of Christian musicians perhaps aren't as good as they should be, but because they're sincere and saying the right things, according to some people, that's the main thing because musical proficiency is perhaps the sign of carnality or something ... I don't know! [Laughter]

That's just the reflection of our pioneering evangelical tradition where everything has to have a practical utilitarian function. And the problem with art is that it is of no use whatsoever, to be honest with you. Because ... you can't put coal in it. You know what I mean?

I mean the reason art exists and is important is because it exists outside of the mundane and the ordinary and the every day. It exists outside of the practicalities of living and it exists to basically transcend mundane conformity.

And that's what art is for; to move you from one place to another and music should do that. So to me, I think there's an argument to say there's an element of God in almost *all* music and *all* art because it's of God and because God is creative.

BW: No matter who the artist is?

DL: Yes. Because the desire of the artist is to make people see things differently, to think differently, to react, to respond, to just move from this position to that position, from this way of thinking to that way of thinking, perhaps. I think in the church, I don't think we've thought it through as well as we might have.

BW: Was it natural for you to include direct Christian themes in your songs?

DL: Yeah, well I just pretty much tell my own story. I was probably more overt earlier on, in terms of a Christian message, than I am now but...

BW: Well, 'Come to Me' from your latest album is pretty overt.

DL: Yeah, that's not trying to hide anything is it? No, I sort of think, 'This is who I am.' You're just there to tell your story, you know? I mean, I know not all songwriters are autobiographical but it occurred to me years ago that if you tell your own story, people can't come up to you and go, 'You got that wrong!' Because it's your story. And if you go to an audience and say, 'Well, this is how it is for *me*. This is *my* story,' they're quite open to it. They don't mind.

BW: Do you think a Christian message has hampered any commercial success?

DL: Oh, bound to have! Bound to have. But you can't ... I just don't wanna make anything up, too much.

BW: You don't have to make it up but, for example, you do the socio-political type songs very well.

DL: Mmm. Oh well. Maybe that's where I've got it wrong, Brett.

Now you tell me! [Laughter] In the twilight of my career ... suddenly I find out the winning formula.

BW: I just wonder if it goes back to that whole thing that was especially magnified in my life, anyway, that you have this expectation as a Christian musician to sing about certain topics and avoid others.

DL: Yeah. I don't feel that pressure at all, to be honest. I think I did when I first started out writing, but by the time I got to make my first album, I wasn't feeling that pressure. I think I did know that most of my audience and most of my buying public would probably come from within the Christian arena, because that's where I cut my teeth, you know what I mean?

But now, I just write 'em as they come. I don't try and second guess anything and it's just part of who I am, and as I say, it's my own story and music is a good way of documenting it.

If you tell your own story hopefully there's enough common ground for it to resonate with other people. I mean, I know secular critics who have said 'Come to Me' is a beautiful song, you know? They may not subscribe to its message particularly. George Harrison would write a Buddhist song and it would still be a lovely song. I was at church on Sunday and somebody was playing 'My Sweet Lord' as background music! [Laughter]

BW: It's a great melody! I just can't sing along to the Hare Krishna bit. But similarly, I think it would be strange for someone to hear 'Come to Me' – even if they're an atheist – and not be moved by just the *music*.

DL: Yeah, well that's the thing about music; it's not just about the lyrical sentiment, there's the whole emotive content of the music. When we run out of things to say, that's when God gives us music.

BW: 'A Bad Song Everyday' suggests that, right from the start, you had a certain drive and tenacity towards being a serious songwriter.

DL: Well, you know when you first start out you need other people to tell you whether you're doing any good or not? It's a bit like when I was art teaching, the kids wanted to know two things, basically, about their work: 'Is it finished and is it any good?' [Laughter]

And when you're young you certainly do rely on other people's input and opinion, but eventually you develop a self-critical faculty and you know whether it's any good or not. You know whether you're on the money or not and so you try not to allow bad stuff to pass muster.

I mean, I don't know whether I was that driven or not. I've always been driven by the *work* not by the trappings of the work, like the business of music. I mean, I'm hopeless at that. I've sort of got an aversion to the whole rock-star thingy, but I might be rationalising my lack of success in this field.

BW: I want to talk about your success soon, but it's just the fact that you *did* it and still continue to do so that separates you from other singer/songwriters who might write a song once a year. If you're doing it every day, and some of them might be bad songs, the writing is only going to get better over time.

DL: As I say, you're gonna hit pay dirt at some point. It's just like any discipline whether it's sport or whatever it is, you just have to work at it. It *is* a discipline.

BW: Sure, but I think for a lot of so-called songwriters, they might go to their guitar every month, if they're lucky, and expect greatness to automatically flow out of that one session. And whatever does flow out is 'sent from above' and therefore it better be left untouched, without critique, because that's their 'art'.

DL: Well, I do try to be reasonably disciplined. I've fallen by the wayside a bit in recent years because of events, but where I live now, I've set it up so I don't have any excuses not to do work. That's with the music and with the art work. I've got dedicated spaces to do it.

I've got all my gear out ready to go so I'm not saying, 'Oh, I can't be bothered getting the guitar out from under the bed.' So it's there. And you sort of have to trick yourself into working and into coming up with ideas because it is sort of like hard work sometimes. It's not therapy. You don't just walk around with blank bits of paper hoping for words to fall out of the sky.

I mean, that whole divine inspiration thing, I don't discount it for a second, but it has to be coupled with a degree of personal discipline and working at your craft, and that applies to whether you're just a player, or whether you're a words person. You have to work at the craft. But art is not always about craft. There's always that indefinable something that makes it jump away from just being a journeyman.

Suddenly there's the art component and that's pretty hard to put your finger on, but it's that element of transcendent truth that somehow comes through and you sort of know it when you see it or hear it. But art doesn't just happen in a vacuum. It happens because someone has disciplined themselves to write all those bad songs, you know?

BW: That reminds me of the joke you've said at gigs about songwriters who announce their next song as 'one that God gave me'. Your response is, 'Well, I know why He gave it to you. Because He didn't want it for Himself!' [Laughter]

Let's talk about the early years of your nascent career, prior to your first album *Mixed Blessings* (1986.) There must have been a point where you thought, 'I'm gonna *do* this! I'm gonna get some gigs, write good songs and record an album!'

DL: Yeah, well I'd been doing the solo thing for quite a bit and my mate, Kevin Adair had started an organisation called Someone Up There and they basically were just setting up gigs for bands around town in non-church environments.

They hired a theatre. I think they did some at the art gallery; unusual places perhaps. Certainly not places where you'd normally go and hear Christian music like in a church. Most of the time he would have two or three bands on the bill and he would ask me to come and play and I would sort of play between two bands while they were setting up for the second one, because it's just me and the guitar so it's easy-peasy.

Eventually, Kevin approached me and asked me if I would like to make an album. And that's how Someone Up There Records started, with my first album. We were very fortunate when we were younger as there were a lot of pretty sympathetic, empathetic venues to play at within the church itself. There were several after evening-church coffee bars around town where we would play quite regularly. YFC was an organisation that would have monthly Town Hall events that I would play at occasionally.

Certain people at the time were writing scripts for certain events that were going on. You know, plays, musical things. People like the Bradley brothers and people like John Hawkesby, the newsreader. He was a bit of a [Bob] Dylan freak, and he was responsible for setting up some after-church thing in Ellerslie.

Anyway, eventually you get a chance to record and your first album is kind of like a 'greatest hits' before you've had any because it represents perhaps a decade of writing. So you're putting out all the songs that have worked and gone well and so it's just this big, long incohesive mess. [Laughter]

First albums don't often sit together very well as a conceptual idea because the songs are often written over a long, protracted period of time. Second and third albums are often more compressed in their thinking because the songs are written in a short timeframe. So eventually it came out. The rest is history!

I'm still singing some of those songs 30-something years later, you know? Which is good. And I'm not singing them because there's an expectation … it's not like I had hits with any of them. [Laughter] But people still seem to enjoy those songs.

BW: It would be pretty rare for a Derek Lind gig to not feature songs from the album like 'Rusty Nail' or 'A Man Like Me', perhaps 'Wasteland' if you had a backing band. They're signature songs for you. Did you have any idea at the time that you might be singing those songs 30 years later?

DL: No, well you don't think 30 years later about anything do you?

BW: Perhaps not. But you didn't think this could be the big break?

DL: Not really. No, I wasn't that delusional. [Laughter]

Let's Back Up a Bit

BW: When did you meet Ra?

DL: I met her at my church.

BW: Ngaire Ave?

DL: Ngaire Avenue Bible Chapel. We started dating New Year's Eve … must have been 1973. Got married in '78. I was finishing high school when we started going out. She was 16, I was 17.

BW: And she sang on quite a few of your albums.

DL: Yeah, she sang on all the ones that I had backing vocals on. I think the last three albums haven't had any backing vocals.

BW: Yeah, and I want to talk about that a little later. But did she ever have her own musical aspirations?

DL: Um, oh no. She was just really supportive of me really. I mean, there was music she obviously liked. She loved Emmylou Harris and a lot of the female singer/songwriter types. We sort of grew up with music together. But Ra was great because she wasn't the greatest singer in the world, but she had a nice honesty and unaffected-ness to her voice, which I kind of liked.

I think it's a good quality to have as a backing vocalist because you're not the gig, you're not the act. You want voices that can blend in, but some backing vocalists don't understand that concept particularly well and it becomes this sort of competitive thing about who can hold the note longer. Do a bit of vocal acrobatics. But the idea is to just sort of sit in there and … you know? She was pretty good at that.

Derek Lind

BW: Your song 'Graveyard Shift' (12 *Good Hours of Daylight*, 2002) is clearly about her. What was her occupation?

DL: Yeah, she had a lot of different jobs but at that time she was working a graveyard shift at Tip Top, I think.

DEREK & Ra LIND - FROM a WEE WHILE aGO.

I was a high school teacher, which I started the year after we got married, and I taught for ten years.

At the end of '89, having toured a bit and releasing a few more albums, I quit. So Ra sort of held us together a lot financially, and that involved quite a few big sacrifices on her part taking on jobs.

I mean, to my credit, and to her credit, she didn't go out into the workforce again until our middle child was 15 years old. So she was a stay-at-home mum for all of the kids' childhoods and early teenage years.

How we managed to do that, I'm not sure, but when I was in full-time music she was working a lot and that was when she was doing the graveyard shift, coming home at eight in the morning, that sort of thing. Which is hard going. It's a pretty hard lifestyle financially doing this stuff.

BW: Considering your work ethic towards developing your craft, which you've downplayed a bit, I think most singer/songwriters seek a bit of acclaim, if not from critics, then certainly at least from their peers. They want to be respected as a songwriter.

You have ticked that box several times over the years including your most recent album, *Solo* (2015). Do you remember thinking along the lines of, 'Wouldn't it be great if they mention my name in the same breath as John Prine,' or whichever one of your heroes' names you want to insert there?

DL: Yeah, of course! You *have* to have a degree of ego to be in this game, you gotta understand that. You can't be in denial of that. I mean, the fact that you stand up on a stage in front of a bunch of people and do something, requires a fairly healthy ego.

But you don't do it to get that ego massaged, that shouldn't be your primary motivator. It *is* nice to have the respect of your peers, it *is* nice to get good reviews, and I'm pretty lucky in that regard, I've done pretty well. It hasn't manifested itself at the box office, so to speak. [Laughter]

BW: If your commercial success was equivalent to the critical success you've received, then you would be a multi-millionaire…

DL: I don't know.

BW: …over and over.

DL: Who knows? Um … I don't know. It would be nice to have a *piece* of that action. [Laughter] But it hasn't happened. I have been fairly well treated by the critics and we've always put our music out in the public arena. I've never really made music for the Christian music industry, as such. I just try and make music that anyone can listen to, hopefully.

I'm not trying to pander or cater to any one specific market, I just sit and make music that I hope people will get something from and it just goes into the world. So we're happy for the *New Zealand Herald* or whatever to take a copy and see what they think of it. I mean, I still get lumbered with the label 'Christian artist' sometimes, with the implication that that's some sort of handicap I carry with me. [Laughter]

Well, people just like to put you in a box in terms of style or category or... Anyway, I don't care, I'm not embarrassed about it.

BW: Well, your faith is right there in your songs. You could've avoided that. Not abandoned your faith but left it out of your songs.

DL: Well, you see I've always been a fairly independent person in terms of not having record company executives breathing down my neck saying, 'You can't talk about this stuff. It would be commercial disaster.' So I've always maintained a fair degree of commercial independence and the secret to that is to keep control of your product as much as you can. I was gonna say another secret is to have a working wife, but... [Laughter]

I've never had that sort of pressure put on me such as, 'Derek, you need to write more funny songs on the next album.' Pretty much, I've had free artistic reign and because I've never really sought to go with a major record label, that hasn't been an issue.

But that could be why also I haven't achieved a great deal of commercial success, but I think I'd rather have artistic freedom than to be some sort of commodity. You know, the moment anything is commodified it basically becomes artistically cheapened, and the same applies to Christian music in terms of the moment a faith becomes a marketable commodity, the thing becomes weakened and diminished somehow.

BW: Yeah, I get that. I guess any commercially successful artist who is similar to you might have the added advantage of living in America where the market is significantly bigger.

DL: You can almost be a cult figure in America and still make a pretty good living simply because of the population. But having said that, some of my songwriters I admire, like John Prine, he was with a major record label, he's not a household name obviously, but highly critically respected.

But he said the first royalty cheque he ever got from a record company was when he formed his own record company and wrote the cheque himself! [Laughter]

So it can look like they're successful, but the artist actually pays for all of that publicity and promotion. The record company might be doing the work, but it's the artist that's paying for it. They might have some notoriety, they might have some public standing, but they're no better off than me, possibly. In my obscurity, financially I might even be better off, who knows?

BW: You actually address this topic on your third album, *Slippery Ground* (1990):

> Some people get their songs on the airwaves / To embrace the shadow of success / My elevation is to bargain-bin status / Will I never get to live a life of excess?

DL: Did I write that? [Laughter] Well, it's kind of a tongue-in-cheek lyric really, you know...

BW: Well, I think it's a fantastic lyric but it seems like, by that stage, you were resigned to the fact that the type of songs you write were never going to bring you any sort of fortune. I mean the song's called 'Where I Want to Be' for goodness sake! As if you'd reject commercial success, even if it did come your way.

DL: Yeah. I guess I saw the writing on the wall. If you're gonna write the sort of stuff I was writing the chances of financial success are pretty slim.

BW: The song continues with:

> Some people never know the struggle / That beauty and truth require / I want to look into the eye of God / And know my Maker's desire.

That's a great lyric. But it bothers me a little bit that all of your critical acclaim hasn't transpired into the equivalent value in terms of commercial success.

DL: Yeah, well … I mean sometimes you think it just doesn't seem very fair but … you know… I… you can't get too… I mean, again I care about the *work*. So if the work is acknowledged as being okay, that's kind of good because the work isn't gonna go away, you know? It might have some posthumous success, Brett. [Laughter]

BW: 'God of Plenty' from *Strange Logic* (1988), takes an interesting angle about materialism:

> God of plenty / My life is empty / I don't want much / I just want more / Fill it up / Don't threaten me with the troubles / Of the hungry, the homeless, the poor / Just give me what I want / And I'll promise I'll never worry you no more.

DL: Yeah, well some people took that song literally, unfortunately. Christians. They thought it wasn't tongue-in-cheek. They thought it was a genuine prayer or something. People don't do irony very well sometimes.

Let's Back Up a Bit

BW: Especially in '88.

DL: Yeah. I'm a bit of a shoot-myself-in-the-foot type guy too because I was with American record companies, distributing my stuff anyway, and publishing companies. But the record company sort of went bust, which didn't help me.

And I also wasn't prepared to take my family on the road. The kids were in their early teens. To be honest, you have to tour your backside off over there. I wasn't feeling very comfortable about the Christian industry, and it didn't help when I wrote songs which criticised them. [Laughter] And then expected them to distribute my stuff.

BW: Why didn't you just go with a secular label?

DL: Well, no one asked me. But the label I was on was Christian but, for America, very left of centre Christian in terms of the musicians they took on. So they were people a little bit like me. I can't remember all the details, but it didn't work out. I was with a publishing company in Nashville and after a year or two of trying or not trying, they reached the conclusion that only Derek can do justice to Derek's songs. Which was a bit of a cop-out for 'We didn't do our job.'

BW: 'God of Plenty' is probably quite a good tie in with your partnership with Tearfund. When did that start?

DL: Well, '88 was when I did my first major tour with them around the country. I'd obviously finished the album before that. I had done stuff with them a few years prior. I would say about '86 on.

They used to bring artists from overseas to promote their

work and I did a few support slots and things like that. And when I started with them it was really just a husband and wife organisation. Very small. And so over the years it's grown quite markedly. I've done less work for them in more recent years but we have a long-standing relationship and we're still in conversation about doing things.

BW: You basically had a decade to work up to *Mixed Blessings*, and then you released the follow-up, *Strange Logic* (1988), two years later. Did you feel any pressure to come up with the goods in two years?

DL: Well, no. I was pretty prolific then, I think. I had the bit between my teeth, you know? And I think that's typical of when you're younger too; you seem to knock out the work and there's probably a little less self-criticism going on than there might be as you get older.

You're a little less discerning so a little bit of rubbish comes down the pike. But I thought that second album was quite good, actually. I'm pretty pleased with all my albums, you know, without showing off. I mean, I think they hold up okay because I haven't tried to be too gimmicky sound-wise with them. I've always stuck, pretty much, with traditional instrumentation, you know what I mean?

BW: Yeah, the production can date an album. The title track says:

> It's a strange logic / It's a strange irony / Living in a world where people build weapons for security.

That is such a timeless theme especially considering the current situation in the USA with gun control, or lack of. This is over 30 years after you wrote that song. Was there a certain event that sparked that song?

DL: I can't really remember. Probably. There's always something going on in that regard, isn't there? I mean, the whole nuclear proliferation thing, it's kind of like a big pissing contest. 'I've got more bombs than you have!' 'Oh well, we'll make some more then!'

That's about the level of mentality that goes on, you know? We could decimate the planet a dozen times over, I'm sure, with all the stuff that's stockpiled. You don't want to be too hard on the States, but it seems to be a country that is governed by fear. It seems to be what wins or loses elections. Trying to create that sense of foreboding or something.

To think that exacerbating the number of arms and making them more readily available is somehow going to make a place safer, it *is* a strange logic, to me anyway. And the facts seem to bear it out.

BW: The liner notes of your 'best of' album mention that the budget was bigger for *Slippery Ground* and that it was released in America but 'no one bought it'. You've just mentioned that you didn't want to tour it...

DL: Yeah ... not if you're trying to raise a family. Maybe I was too scared. I wasn't prepared to spend three or four months on my own. I wasn't convinced about the whole idea of the Christian music industry. Because in America, particularly at that time, it could be different now, but there was a very clear distinction in the same way that you're either a Republican or a Democrat, you're either a Christian musician or you're a secular musician.

In New Zealand, it's too small. You can have a lot of overlap, you know? Because there's only so many gigs and people might be in more than one band so there's not that same clear division. The music I loved the most came from outside of the Christian arena.

In my opinion, most of the Christian music was a pale imitation of something that had already happened, and I still subscribe to that a little bit. You know, the moment you get an indie-folk act or a ... I don't know ... I'm trying to think of an example ... but suddenly you'll find a Christian equivalent. Whether it's Mumford & Sons, suddenly you get a whole ... you know ... at one point everyone sounded like Coldplay. The Edge [guitarist for U2] has got a lot to answer for, for all of these chimey worship songs. [Laughter]

BW: He sure does! But do you think you're exempt from people seeing you as the Christian equivalent of Neil Young (or insert name of white male secular singer/songwriter here)?

DL: I think pretty much all songwriters wear their musical influences loudly on their sleeves, especially when they are starting out. I'm sure I did. I think over time your personal style sorts itself out and for myself, I think I'm mining a musical seam which keeps me sustained and stimulated.

I don't have any great desire to imitate a current trend or style in order to appear 'relevant', whatever that means. What I'm saying is the Christian music industry tends to be more reactionary and tends to imitate, with a Christian twist and often a little after the fact, the prevailing trends in the secular, commercialised, commodified world.

But the thing that troubles me is, back in the day, the church was the chief patronage of the greatest art that was ever made

Let's Back Up a Bit

and was the forerunner. Now we just sort of come along and mildly mimic what's happened a year and a half ago in the real world. There's no real great innovation. Or there may be but it's not getting any attention.

I think, in the new world anyway, the church in its infancy has been that very practical, very utilitarian sort of church where the buildings are very functional, there's no room for ornamentation, there's no room for fear of graven imagery implications, there's no frivolity. Everything's very austere and practical and everything has to have a function.

We're slowly changing and we're starting to get an appreciation for our own culture, for our own music, for our films, you know? There's less of that cultural cringe. But in the church, there's still a wee bit of that pioneering approach so we've demystified everything. So there's no room for the mystery of the Gospel or the mystery of the incarnations.

But, you know, I think we might get there. We're getting there. Well, certain people have embraced that side of things a lot more and the arts have a much wider platform, and there's a better understanding of the term 'the arts' in a wider spectrum. People are using moving images and installations just to help people get to this point of transcendence. We get scared of words like 'transcendence' and 'mystery' because they invoke some sort of New Age ... you know ... but there *is* a mystery and there *is* a transcendence to the whole story of the Gospel.

BW: If the first three albums have moments of angst and production values that almost place you as the frontman for your own rock band, then *Stations* (1994) is the start of another trilogy of albums with a stripped back sound and a conversational tone. Was it a conscious decision to go for a different sound?

DL: I think so. I wanted to make music in a more intimate setting and, at the time, digital technology had come in and so you weren't restricted to the studios. So I did a lot of that album at home on my own, and my producer at the time, Steve Garden, fixed everything up later and I did some stuff in the studio too.

But I think I sensed in myself that the songs were moving in a more intimate direction. I think I was also influenced a lot by recordings like Bruce Springsteen's *Nebraska* and Bob Dylan's *Oh Mercy!* They just had some lovely, intimate sort of things going on and I was just struck by the power of some of those records, which were very simple production-wise, and it came down to the songs. I mean, one of the reasons there's a lot of production on some albums is because the songs aren't so good, to be honest with you. They're just polishing them up!

I didn't feel that I was trying to hide anything too much with the bigger production on *Slippery Ground*, for example, but a good song should be able to survive in a very simple setting with a very simple arrangement. And it was probably a reflection of what I was listening to and what I could afford to do. I didn't have the financial backing that I had for the other ones. It was a more appropriate artistic context in which to record the songs I was writing.

But the albums have become more personal and more intimate and whilst the last album [*Solo*] we did in a very good studio [Roundhead Studios] with very good gear, that was just there to try and capture the degree of fidelity on a bunch of simple, very direct songs.

We weren't using any of the studio's wizardry. We were just trying to find somewhere where we could play essentially live that would faithfully duplicate what was happening in the room, and that studio was one of the few in town that could do that.

Let's Back Up a Bit

BW: One of the highlights from *Stations* is 'Sacred Conversation', not just for the fantastic performance by Brendan Power on harmonica, but the lyric contains a reasonable amount of ambiguity:

> Turn the radio on / It's A.M. or nothing / Talkback or gospel / Stations of the cross / And they're grinning it or bearing it / But there is no passion / So I turn it off.

That appears to be a comment on a disingenuous moment on Christian radio...

DL: Well, I don't know if it was a *moment*... [Laughter] It's just the passionless of a lot of Christian radio. I mean I could say the passionless of a lot of Christian music, but that's not fair. But what the radio stations choose to play is...

BW: It has to be at a certain commercial level I guess...

DL: I guess so. But, as I say, I'm not even sure what defines Christian music let alone Christian radio. It's a bit of an alien life-form, to me. The whole thing, to be honest. I've always felt like a bit of a stranger to it and that's part of what stymied my career, I think, is that I've never felt a strong allegiance to the Christian industry or the secular industry. I sort of do the splits a wee bit, you know what I mean?

BW: Has Christian radio ever picked up on your songs?

DL: Yeah. I mean they try and find *something*. [Laughter] But it's not going to be on high rotation I suspect. No, they do their best. They'll always try and find room for an interview or something if I've got something coming up. I mean, they're very good, but the overreaching sort of feeling I get is … well, they're just not playing anything I particularly want to listen to.

I could be wrong, but my feeling is that they're sort of playing music for people that subscribe to their station, their supporters. That's the demographic so that's what we'll give them. I don't want to be too scathing of it but a lot of resource and money goes into these things, from generous people, and I'm not too sure how effective it is and that's the other issue; the way they justify their existence is they'll say, 'Well, we programme to this many people.'

And musicians are the same, 'We sang to this many people. We toured to 70,000 people. We gave out 70 million tracts.' Blah-di-blah-di-blah. And so you have to quantify your spiritual successful significance or impact in order to convince the generous public to support your organisation.

And again, it's a form of commodification justified by a presentation of a bunch of numbers. I'm not sure how that sits with me. But you don't make a record and hope that no one buys it. It's just the way it's turned out. But it's a commercial entity and you want to get your costs back, if you can. So again you're conflicted all the time.

It's easy to get sucked into some vortex of commercialism, some vortex of consumerism, some vortex of commodification and that becomes dangerous and you lose track of what you're trying to do, which is to be a person of artistic integrity, and personal integrity and hopefully that reflects in your music and hopefully your faith manifests itself in and through it.

BW: 12 *Good Hours of Daylight* (2002) and the follow-up album *Solo* (2015) have a few things in common; sonically, they are similar but also, respectively, they discuss the loss of your

Let's Back Up a Bit

father and your wife, Ra. Both deaths were quite sudden too, if I'm not mistaken.

DL: Dad's was pretty quick, yeah. They discovered he had a rather massive brain tumour and I think from that point to the point where he died was less than a month. So not much warning there. And even less so with Ra. No warning whatsoever.

BW: And going back to that song, 'A Bad Song Everyday', it mentions how you felt the expectation to write a song in tribute to your father and the guilt you felt when nothing came. Eventually something did come because 'What Came Natural' addresses him directly. Did you have similar feelings after Ra passed away?

DL: Oh, that's a bit different again. No, no I didn't really because, while I was numb, I had no feelings. I was just in a bit of a dazed glaze. Yeah, I was just pretty much immobilised really. But eventually a few songs started to trickle out. You can't not go through something that traumatic and not bear witness to it somehow, and if music is what you do ... you know what I mean?

BW: I probably don't know what you mean because I haven't gone through that.

DL: No. But I knew at some point I would respond, but the best I could do in the first six or eight months after was just to set myself up in such a way that when I got my mojo back I'd be ready to go.

So I got all my gear and hung it up in my music room so I could access everything. I did silly things like, I've got quite a few guitars so I had them all up on hangers all around the walls, and thought, 'What if I die and no one knows which case belongs to which guitar?' So you do silly things. You go through and you put gaffer tape on the cases and say which case belongs to what.

So I set myself up so that if I felt like writing, I *could* do it. And it was the same in the studio. I bought paint, materials, boards, all the stuff you need to make pictures, and just set it up. Didn't do anything. That was what I could do, at the time, and that was about all. I couldn't actually commit to writing or painting, but I knew eventually it would pass, so I did what I could practically do.

BW: Did someone suggest for you to do that or did it come off your own bat?

DL: It came off my own bat. I mean it was a bit illogical, you know, me fussing about with guitar cases in case I die. But it's becoming aware of your own mortality. And you tend to think that way. Once I got this project underway [recording *Solo*] I remember panicking that I might die before I documented this stuff. So what I did was I very quickly demoed the songs so that I thought, 'At least, if I die...' [Laughs] This is the stupid way you think, 'If I die, at least I've got these rough demos. They might be able to do something with them.' And once that happened, I think I was okay.

But the whole Kickstarter thing [crowd-sourced funding for the recording] for the new album, that was a two-pronged form of motivation. Firstly to raise the money for the album, and to reward the people that donated to the album, it was suggested that I do some little paintings on paper. So it made me start painting again. It got me into the studio again, which was a good thing for me. You know, I had to work quite hard.

Let's Back Up a Bit

BW: And that album is full of powerful songs that any songwriter or anyone who admires the craft of a well-written song would be in awe of. Some of them deal with loss and raw heartache. And I remember saying to you once that of course you would trade those songs in an instant if it meant...

DL: ...getting her back.

BW: Are you able to talk about the inevitable struggle of spending time crafting these songs, developing them as you would with any other song, while at the same time having the songs conjure up feelings and emotions that are hard to deal with?

DL: Well, I thought I'm best to try and be fairly direct emotionally and lyrically rather than imply stuff and disguise stuff behind words. So it was a fairly direct emotional response in some of the songs and they're very simple, chordally, structurally and lyrically. There's nothing too cryptic about a lot of the songs. I do work very hard at the craft of making it seem very simple and off-hand, but I've spent a lot of time on getting those words right.

The initial response might be, you know, just blurt it out, but then you sit there and you refine it and make subtle changes. It's quite hard to write simply and to reduce it down to the bare bones with just the right words. It should sound like the most normal thing possible. Some of them I didn't use the band at all. I just did them on my own to keep them as bare as I possibly could.

Some of them screamed, 'Put a harmony on it!' You could stack harmonies on it, you could do this, you could do that. But I thought sometimes you just gotta pare it right back to get to the bare bones and the heart of the matter. So they were quite hard to record and sometimes they're a bit hard to perform. Sometimes they just catch you off guard and you find yourself struggling to get through them.

But I don't worry too much about that. I mean, I can't watch a *Bambi* film without crying my eyes out these days. [Laughter] It just comes with the territory, so I just roll with the punches, you know? That's just the nature of grieving I think. You just got to relax and not worry about it. Yeah.

BW: Finally, Dave White has affectionately referred to you as 'the Godfather of Contemporary Christian Music in New Zealand'. Do you have any thoughts on your contribution to music in New Zealand?

DL: I don't know. Well, I suppose I did a bit of a Larry Norman-ish sort of thing in New Zealand.

BW: There wouldn't have been many people at the time doing what you were doing. Or am I wrong?

DL: No. Well, there were people like Mark Laurent and Guy [Wishart] of course. I think Guy released an album before I did, but perhaps he didn't have quite the same profile I guess in the Christian scene. I don't know. I have no idea. But I was just trying to write normal music really. You know, you're not trying to pioneer anything but … um …

BW: Either people don't admit it, or they just don't think at the time…

DL: No, you don't. You don't have the objectivity that others might have. But I wasn't on a mission or anything. There was

Let's Back Up a Bit

no manifesto. I was just doing the stuff that I could stand. I was a Christian, but most of my influences came from outside of Christendom and I just incorporated those elements I guess.

BW: Is it easier to look back in hindsight and perhaps realise that what you were doing was a little unique back in the day?

DL: Well, there weren't a lot of us doing anything much, you know? I mean, now everyone's in a band. I think also, I've stuck at it. I've stuck to my guns a little more.

You know, a lot of people, they had their day in the sun, and they've retired [from music] and got sensible lives. I guess I probably influenced a few younger people like Dave White a bit, but [cue a rather cheeky grin] I'll let other people decide what giant shadow I have cast, Brett.

Derek Lind is an artist and singer/songwriter who lives in a small settlement called Parau – halfway between Huia and Titirangi in the Waitākere Ranges, Auckland. He is the father of three adult children and has five grandchildren. His music can be sourced online or via his website: www.dereklind.com

DAVID & DALE GARRATT

The inclusion of David and Dale Garratt is a little unique in this book as most other artists here didn't necessarily write their music for the church to sing.

It was either intended as entertainment or ministry (or both). But worship music is certainly significant in a discussion on Christian music and the Garratts are most significant in terms of introducing a new style of praise and worship music, not only in New Zealand, but in many parts of the globe.

Consider the words of author, Tim Dowley in his book *Christian Music: A Global History* as he discusses 'new hymns, praise songs, and other forms of congregational song in popular styles' coming out of Australia and New Zealand in the mid-1960s and early 1970s:

> Most successful of these was husband-and-wife team, David and Dale Garrett [sic] from New Zealand who wrote and compiled the Scripture in Song (1979-1988) song books that became popular worldwide. While drawing on material from the USA and UK, they also promoted local song-writers and exposed their work to the global audience, paving the way for the wealth of material produced in this region at the end of the twentieth century.

DAVID & DALE GARRATT.

Those song books were certainly popular in the church I grew up in, the Hamilton Apostolic Church (later known as Eastside Church, even later known as Activate Church).

I remember singing songs from those books most often accompanied by my mum on organ and, later, my brother, Ross, on clarinet. They both favoured the flat keys, B flat being the most popular (though Mum would identify this as 'two flats').

Everyone colloquially referred to these song books as 'the brown and blue books' for obvious reasons. Officially, these are respectively titled *Scripture and Song: Volume One – Songs of Praise* and *Scripture and Song: Volume Two – Songs of the Kingdom* but 'the brown and blue books' was way catchier. To this very day I can recall, without looking, that #22 in the brown book was the bouncy 'He is My Everything'.

Number 1 in the blue book was the anthemic 'Majesty'. Of course, it always helps to have the word 'anthem' in the lyrics of the song in order for it to be anthemic. '... His anthem raaaaiise...' That's just basic song-writing. While I remember many of the songs from *Scripture and Song: Book Three – Songs of the Nations* (or 'the yellow book' if you will), I don't recall holding a yellow book in my pre-teen hands. I have to put this down to the fact that, by then, the church had progressed to fancy new technology called the Overhead Projector or OHP for short (probably should be OP as 'overhead' is one word).

This 'advanced' machinery rendered reading songs from a book old-fashioned. From now on, people, heads will no longer be buried in books but raised towards the almighty glow of the OP while singing 'Lift Up Your Heads' (#13 in the blue book – key of A flat – four flats, Mum).

THE HAMILTON APOSTOLIC CHURCH MUSIC TEAM MID-'80S WITH MY BROTHER ROSS WILSON ON THE CLARINET AND MUM (MARGARET WILSON) ON THE ORGAN. NOTE SHE IS PLAYING FROM 'THE BROWN AND BLUE BOOKS'.

Let's Back Up a Bit

My conversation with David Garratt took place during their stay in the USA in a place called Newbury Park, a small area within Thousand Oaks, less than 90 minutes north of Los Angeles. This was proving to be a good place for them to hibernate while Dale put the finishing touches on her book, *Please Help Yourself*.

But more importantly, David tells me, they wanted to catch up with their close friends Jimmy and Carol Owens, who they have known since their first trip to the US in the 1970s. Talk about name-dropping! Among other achievements, the Owens wrote several popular Christian musicals in the 1970s such as *Come Together*, though their children's album, *Ants'hillvania* from 1981 resonates with me more. Great record. They are also the parents of well-known contemporary Christian singer, Jamie Owens-Collins and pastor Buddy Owens.

I began my chat with David by reading out the Tim Dowley quote previously mentioned and wanted to know how he would respond to the notion of being a pioneer of a new style of worship music.

David Garratt: Yes, I don't doubt that we did pioneer something because in 1968 we actually put our first album out that year, which was before anyone else did as far as I'm aware. Then in the 1970s we went to the States and we met with Maranatha Music and we met with John Wimber who started Vineyard, and later on we went to England and met with the Kingsway people [Kingsway Communications] and then later on again with Integrity Music, and so we got around the main American and English publishers.

It was interesting that the Holy Spirit did begin something

that spread a long way. I'm not saying that it spread because of us at all, but it actually did begin something in New Zealand and God really did something with us as non-musicians that was somewhat unique because we just felt, right back at that stage, that He was wanting songs that are sung to Him and He was wanting us to encourage His people to worship and to learn His Word.

And so because we're not musicians, we saw the music as being something which would carry the message. But at the same time we realised that there were certain styles of music and there were certain ways music was put into song that meant that people would or would not remember, because the memorisation was the key factor with what we were doing.

We weren't singing songs just to entertain people, we were singing songs so when they went home the melody would stick with them, and the words would too, and over the years I've had many responses from people who still remember the songs.

And really the whole point of it was actually a training thing, it was a teaching situation. I have to say it pretty well wasn't anything like what you would see today. I'm saying that mainly because, and I found this out later on when I went to Integrity Music in the 1980s, I realised then that all the songs these days are written by musicians and the music is a really important factor to them. In fact, it seems to me a lot more important than the lyrics themselves. That's my impression of it. And also, and it's certainly not a universal statement, I hear some really good songs, but it seems to me, fairly objectively, that songs are written *for* musicians. They're written for their peers.

The music has often become the master when it should serve the words. Whereas we were writing songs for people that weren't musicians at all. We were writing songs for people so they could learn the Word of God. Although 'worship' is what is sort of used in a very broad sense of the word these days, I would say probably 75 percent of the songs we wrote – and of Scripture in Song we had about 450 of them – were songs that I would describe as teaching songs.

In other words, they were taking Scriptures, things that we felt God was wanting to say at a particular time, and putting them to music; putting them out there so that people would learn the principles. And this is something that I marvel at a bit; music is such a powerful medium and yet I wonder how many people, especially Christian musicians and worship leaders, actually realise how powerful it is.

When I say 'powerful', I mean powerful in terms of getting something of what you're wanting to sing into the hearts of people. I don't even know if that answers your question because I can't even remember it. [Laughter]

Brett Wilson: Well, it more than answers my question. It's interesting how you say you weren't musicians, yet God used you in a significant way with music. What were you and Dale doing before Scripture in Song and before it became this huge thing?

DG: We were married in Auckland in 1964, and right at that stage I got a job at the Bell Tea company in Dunedin. So for the next three years we were in Dunedin.

Prior to going to Dunedin, we were involved in singing in different situations; with YFC, with Open Air Campaigners and with a little radio station in Birkdale in Auckland, where they would record songs and teachings to send to overseas radio programmes.

But just before we got married and travelled south, we felt God told us to stop what we were doing in terms of singing because He wanted to give us something more effective. So we went down there and no one knew us in Dunedin, so there was no one to question because we used to get a lot of calls from people to come and sing at events. In those days the quality of music and musicianship was low enough that they asked us to come. [Laughter]

Anyway, as we arrived back in Auckland in 1967, the Charismatic Movement was really beginning to take place in New Zealand. Not only in New Zealand but around the world. It actually started prior to that in other places, but God started to reveal something about the Holy Spirit to people around the world in the 1950s and the 1960s. We weren't aware of it.

I was brought up in a Brethren church in Wellington and Dale was brought up in a completely non-religious situation and, when we came to Auckland, Derek Prince came out from America and did some teaching and we were asked to sing. It was epic for us because after three years of waiting and obeying God He was now saying, 'Sing again'. This situation is described well in Dale's book, *Please Help Yourself*.

It was during those meetings that we began to hear little choruses that we hadn't heard before. At that stage everyone was pretty much singing hymns and the churches were using a piano and an organ on different sides of the room and they never seemed to relate to each other at all. So we thought why don't we just put a little album together of these new songs and put it out there because there were a lot of people who couldn't go to these meetings. That really was the thought.

Dale had a cousin who was a guitarist, a non-Christian, we both had a friend who was a drummer who had come to God, and he had a mate who played piano who came from the pub scene. So we went to a studio and in four hours we completed an album of nine songs, put them on a little EP, which we simply titled, *Scripture in Song*.

Let's Back Up a Bit

Amazingly, it was the music for the time, although we didn't realise that, and people began to buy it. We were packing it ourselves, of course. I had a sister in Australia who asked us to send some over. I sent over a couple of hundred and she needed more. Also at that stage, we had two little kids and we decided we'd write some songs for children along the same lines. We did three children's albums around 1969-1971 because we wanted to teach our kids about the Word of God and we were beginning to realise that music was the best way to do that.

But then Dale began writing as well as other people, and in 1972 we recorded a double album at Stebbing Studios in Auckland. We called it *Prepare Ye the Way*; we were still into King James English in those days. That sold as a platinum album in New Zealand and sold hugely around the world in English-speaking countries.

We sold in South Africa, England, Australia, United States and then other places like Singapore and other parts of Europe as well. So we found ourselves in this situation and for some reason it never seemed a big deal, although to sell 100,000 albums today would be a big deal. But um... we sold a lot of albums.

BW: Wow.

DG: Yeah. Because of what was going on in the Spirit, and because there were things spontaneously happening around the world where God was opening the eyes of His people to the reality of the gifts of the Spirit, and because the music that we were putting out related to that. That's the reason it went so well because we've never been good promoters and we've never actually grown much.

David & Dale Garratt

BW: What do you mean you haven't grown much?

DG: Well, other companies became large companies. Integrity Music became very big in the 1980s. Vineyard became pretty big. Kingsway Music has been sold to the publishing company, David C. Cook, as well as Integrity. [Pauses]

It's funny really because I look back and all I'm talking to you about is history. But what I'm really interested in is where I'm going. I don't know whether you're interested in that. I am, but it doesn't necessarily cover what you want to write about and that's fine.

BW: Well, I am interested in that and I'm sure others will be too. I do intend to discuss your present, but your history is an important story to Christian music in New Zealand.

DG: Okay. Well, what do you want to talk about then?

BW: Well, I'd be interested to know *how* the songs went around the world. You say it sold so much but how did it exactly go around the world?

DG: Okay. Well, initially through our global travel, which we did every year since about 1974, but then through individual people. We led worship at several events in Tauranga at Christmas time, and these conferences would bring in overseas teachers to speak.

In 1972, we were in Tauranga for the Christmas meeting and Jimmy Moore, an American who would probably not even be known now, came down and he liked what we were doing so much he said, 'I'd like to be able to distribute your albums in the

Let's Back Up a Bit

United States.' He lived in a place called Ruston in Louisiana, so he began to sell right from there.

I don't know the dates of the others, but in the mid-1970s we went to South Africa and we found another man Helge Schnemann who wanted to sell our recordings in South Africa, and he did. And then you may have heard of Arthur Wallis who was a Bible teacher from England. Arthur's brother Peter wanted to handle our recordings in England.

These guys, just individuals, all of whom started from nothing and all of whom sold a lot. In addition to these, Keith Chua in Singapore believed in what we were doing and, most important of all, John Muys set up a company in Australia which became our biggest market outside New Zealand. John is looking to help us now as we look into the future.

In the 1970s we led worship at two fairly major conferences in New Zealand. One was in Palmerston North at a racecourse. It went for three or four years and we led all the worship and 3,000 people would come each year. Just to give you an example of this, around 1978, we did an album that came out of those conferences in Palmerston North. It was called *Praise the Name of Jesus*, a live album recorded on a 4-track with an audience of around 3,000 people.

A friend of ours said 'Let's record this!' And it was so much worse than anything we'd done from a quality point of view that I really didn't know if we should do anything with it. And I still remember asking God about it and He said to me, 'If you put this out it will be like a seed and I will cause it to grow.' Well, Peter Wallis sold 90,000 of those albums in England alone.

BW: Woah!

DG: So it's really remarkable the way God actually does take the foolish things to complete His tasks. We had no natural ability as musicians, as engineers, technicians. We found ourselves working with engineers and I'd say to them, 'I don't like that,' and they'd say, 'Well, what do you want to do?' and I'd say, 'I have no idea what to do. I just don't like the way it is. Try something else.' [Laughter]

So really, over the years, because we've done over 30 albums, we've had to work in situations where so many people we were with, whether they were musicians or technicians or producers or whatever, they've had so much more experience. But because of God's guidance I sort of knew what was right and wasn't right, it was just like that.

Now I'm not saying everything we did was good. I think there were times where, for instance, I allowed an engineer to do something on an album because he had the ability and I felt I didn't. And other times I think, in fact I'm quite sure, I can think of at least one of the albums we did that I didn't think that God ever said to do it; but we did it. So you learn.

In fact, let me back up a wee bit. We did the first album in 1968, as I said. The next year we did another album and the piano player that worked on the first album, who was a non-Christian, said, 'I can do something really good with this.' And we were pretty awed by this guy because he was good and so we allowed him to produce an album for us and it hardly sold at all. And God was saying to us, 'This is My thing. Just trust Me.' [Laughter]

It's so interesting because then we put out the third album, which we did the same as we did the first one, and it began to sell again. So these sorts of little lessons that you learn along the way, of trusting and learning to trust God, have really been, and still are to this very day, vital in our lives.

Because God is saying if you trust in Him, He will direct you.

Let's Back Up a Bit

It's as simple as that. And I think when you're in the midst of creativity it's very easy, if you've got skill in an area, to actually allow the skill to take over from actually trusting God even though you're a believer. It's easy to do, you know?

BW: Wow. That is very cool.

DG: Ah, actually, later on I think we made some mistakes. We put our product with some larger companies in England and in America and they never did as well as when we worked with just a single individual who really believed in what we were doing. It's good to realise why we did what we did and if this is something, hopefully of God, then He needs be involved in every aspect. He really does.

BW: Did you receive any flak from people in the church for the new style of music that you were writing and promoting?

DG: It's a funny thing – it's a good question because actually we didn't.

BW: Really? That wasn't the answer I was expecting!

DG: Except that a retailer we tried to sell to said no one would buy the music. It was probably only a week later he was calling for albums. Mind you, the introduction of drums, electric guitar and bass took a while for people to get used to. And yet other people came to us and said, 'Oh my church is in such a mess! Half of them want to sing your songs and half of them want to sing the old songs!' So they put two styles into their services.

But because our stuff sold very widely in New Zealand, they

were using the books in every denomination. It was pretty widespread, and I think in some respects, regardless of denomination, churches were using our books in one way or another, listening to our songs. The music was the thing that almost united the people, perhaps.

A while ago I was in little Anglican church somewhere out of Huntly and I found our books there, and yet the last one we produced was in 1987 so why they've still got them, I have no idea. The books have been found in the remotest parts of Africa and the Pacific Islands and Europe. We have even found our books in the little painted church in the Big Island of Hawaii.

Dale recalls our drummer coming to her at a big church in Auckland saying he was so discouraged by the people saying drums and guitars were the devil's instruments that he wanted to pack up his drum kit and quit. Dale tried to put out many fires. Maybe people were too scared to speak to me about 'worldly music' as I just didn't hear these things. [Laughter]

BW: These days we have famous faces and celebrities in worship. There's also a lot of copying of what they do. Did it ever enter your head to try and do what someone else was doing or was there less outside influence in that sense?

DG: There was a lot less outside influence. Yes. I still remember being with the company we worked with in Australia, being over there around about 1983 or 1984 and saying to the guy there, 'Other people are doing what we're doing. I'm not a competitor. I'm a pioneer. I don't want to be doing what other people are doing regardless of whether we started it or not.'

We got to the stage where it was almost a comparative thing, in my mind, this was beginning to happen. And because what

Let's Back Up a Bit

DAVID & DALE, MID-'80S.

we did was never professionally great, we couldn't really compete with great singers and great musicians, and quite frankly I didn't want to. It just wasn't a part of what I wanted to do.

And even today, since 1987, I've had a real call from God to work with indigenous people and that's right through to this very day. I was in Japan about a month ago teaching a course on songwriting, which was amazing to me. Last November I was in India, and I'm seeing things now that I'm extremely gratified about and they are still very new. So I don't feel like I'm competing with anyone. I'm just grateful that God continues to give us something to aspire to.

But to address the whole celebrity thing, [pauses] ... gosh!

You just get glimpses. I was in Texas somewhere. I don't know when it was, probably in the 1990s. When Integrity Music started in 1985 they started putting out an album every two months and they never repeated a song. They just gathered songs from all over the place, stuck it on an album and put it out.

And as they started doing this the world got saturated with that style of music, which is the same sort of thing that we were doing before that. I can still remember being in quite a big room and this worship leader, who was leading for this particular Integrity album, came out on stage and everyone just cheered and it just struck me, 'What is this? What are we doing this for?' It really impacted me. One reason it impacted me was I knew the guy and my knowledge of him was he wouldn't have liked that. But this is the way people respond to personality.

BW: A lot of the big producers of worship music these days appear to be producing stars to hang their brand on. And while this is normal practice in mainstream marketing, what do you think about that? Is that something that should be mixed with worship music, or is there tension there?

DG: [Laughter] Well, worship is about giving my attention to God, my love expressed to God and when you talk about worship music – although there's some good stuff coming out of places like Bethel and Hillsong – I don't think God is at all interested in elevating human beings. I think He's interested in us elevating Him. I think He's interested in His own honour.

And I really feel quite sure that quite a lot of these people who are leading worship today are men and women of God, but I think the system has probably grabbed them and made them into something they never would want to be. But it's a very subtle thing, isn't it?

Let's Back Up a Bit

I mean when you think of the temptation of Adam and Eve and realise how easily they seemed to be swayed by the deceiver, is it any wonder that the same doesn't happen today? Of course it does. If you talk about celebrity and worship, you're talking about two quite separate things. I don't think you can put them together successfully.

BW: On a similar topic, if I can get a little personal for a moment, you've sold a lot of albums and song books over the years and with that comes financial success, no doubt. How do you grapple with that? Worship music and financial success. Are you comfortable talking about that?

DG: During our years of recording, writing and publishing we always had enough. Never more than enough. The travel and recordings cost a lot and we always managed to pay or should I say, God always provided for us.

In 1987, God spoke clearly to me about getting to know Māori people and understanding them. He said, 'If you're going to be of any value to Me in the days ahead you need to understand them. You need to understand not just in a superficial way.'

And this, without even learning the language, is what I have tried to do. As I started to investigate, I contacted a friend of mine and, going to a marae, I realised culturally there was a huge gap between us, a huge gulf. And that led me on a whole new journey that's become a passion of mine.

Let me just say this, and I'll go back to your question. A number of weeks ago I felt God say to me when Lucifer was cast out of heaven, he took with him creativity and song and he spread that right throughout the earth.

At the tower of Babel, when the languages were distributed

and the people found their places, they found the treasure of God there already. But they found an enemy with them at the same time, and the enemy distorted all of the goodness of God, which means that indigenous people everywhere have a mixture.

They have a lot of understanding about the Creator. A lot of them have stories about Creation, about the Flood and all sorts of things. But in the middle of it all, just as Satan does, he's distorted that. And the thing I felt deep in me, a little while ago, was God saying, 'I want to hear the worship of My people in their own cultural expressions again because it was stolen, and actually it's Mine.' And I just felt a little touch of God's heart in that, so that's actually largely what I've been involved with since 1993-1994.

In 1994, I went to Alice Springs and stood in front of 200 or 300 Aboriginals and said, 'God wants to hear your didgeridoo and your clapsticks. He wants to hear those things. But the enemy has told you that they're evil because he's used them for his own purposes.'

You know I was there five days and every afternoon I tried to encourage this group, and they just looked at me and wondered what on earth I was talking about. Then on the fifth day – on the Friday, I'll never forget it – two men came in the back of the room and each of them had a piece of plastic piping and they began to play the sound.

And I called them up to the front and when they played the people changed. They heard their own sound you see. They'd been told that the didgeridoo was used by the enemy, therefore they couldn't use it. So when that happened they realised if this can happen in a Christian setting, then God must love us. It just changed everything.

Now in terms of the money. Okay. In 1995 we sold Scripture in Song to Integrity Music and all of a sudden, we had money. So it was really interesting because we had invested in a local property developer, and he lost it for us.

But I think there was something there of God because He didn't want us to rely on the money. But He does want us to have our trust in Him. I realise as I look back on that, 'Gosh! I've got a couple of million dollars. What am I going to do with this?' You know? And then... it's gone. [Laughter mixed with bemusement.]

Well, we didn't actually lose it all, but we probably lost a good two-thirds of it anyway and now we live by faith. But here's the interesting thing: years and years ago both Dale and I felt God say, 'You'll never be without financially. I'm going to look after you.'

Another wonderful thing happened before we lost the funds. We gave a sum to five of the people who, in the beginning, had so willingly and freely given their time and abilities to us.

BW: That's awesome. When did you begin to notice churches shifting away from Scripture in Song, perhaps in favour of other avenues of worship music? Was it a noticeable shift?

DG: Not really, no. As I mentioned to you earlier, I did notice by the mid to late 1980s we were certainly not the only ones in the field and we had to feel that it was right to do another album. It was a progressive thing, I think.

During the 1970s and early part of the 1980s I think Scripture in Song was the leading resource for worship in the churches because we'd put out enough albums and books and they sold well enough to keep that going. Then American and English writers and books became more popular and we became one among a number of others. I guess it was just a progressive thing, really. Because I felt the call of God in a different direction, it didn't really bother me.

We had a 25th anniversary of Scripture in Song in 1993, and we hired the ASB Stadium in Auckland. Over four days we had several thousand people come to events there. It was a pretty big event, but before that time I went around Auckland to every church I could find where the people weren't English speakers first off.

I said, 'We've got this event, please come and bring your dances and songs.' And so from my point of view, it was not so much looking at the last 25 years but looking forward. I think, for a number of people, that was really difficult because they wanted to sing all the old songs but for me the question's always been, 'What is God saying now?' It's always been like that. But that was the event that actually made me decide that Scripture in Song is finished.

An Australian girl at the event got up and read a Scripture from Isaiah 43:18-19 NIV: 'Forget the former things; do not dwell on the past. See, I am doing a new thing!' She had no idea, but I looked at her and I thought, 'Wow. God's actually speaking to me.' And because it had been several years since He'd started to speak to me about the indigenous people, I knew straight away basically what the new thing was.

At our 25th anniversary, Loren Cunningham, founder of YWAM said that in the future it would be said that worship would be known as before Oct One, (what we named the celebration), and after Oct One. Looking at the nation now, and the huge interest in Te Reo Māori [the Māori language], it is easy to understand the truth of his words.

Let's Back Up a Bit

BW: How would you measure your success? What do you want to be remembered for?

DG: I think the main thing, and this is right up to date, is learning to listen to the Holy Spirit. Because it's not that the past is unimportant, but God is really the God of *now*. He's the God of today.

Since 1971 I've been keeping a journal, and for the last number of years I've just typed it up on this computer I'm speaking to you on. This morning, I felt like I should read from Hosea and so I started to read and I just felt God speak to me about Hosea 1 and 2 and how, although it related to Israel, there are so many principles there that related to the way the people of the land are.

And so I just typed it up and sometimes when I type, I'd say, 'Father, what about this?' And I'd just hear something. I'd feel Him answer me. And so that to me means that from my personal point of view, I'm hearing what God's saying now.

My daughter said to me the other day, 'Dad, you're a very simple person.' And I am. I'm a very simple person. I left school as soon as I turned 16 because I was no good academically. But I think the simplicity helped my faith, quite frankly. Because it's helped me say, 'Okay God, I'm listening, I want to hear You.' And the fact is, as Jesus said to the church of Laodecia, 'I'm standing at the door and knocking. If any of you hear My voice, open the door and I will come in. We'll sit down and we'll have a feed together.' I think that is our God and I think that's what He wants from each one of us; to learn, to sit and listen.

David & Dale Garratt

David and Dale Garratt founded Scripture in Song which celebrated its 50th anniversary in 2019. The Garratts are currently writing songs for a younger generation and, just as they did in the past, they are using the musical genres of the day by putting Scripture into song once again.

STEVE APIRANA.

STEVE APIRANA

There will be thousands of Kiwis who know and remember Steve Apirana.

Probably because he visited their church and played his songs and told stories that would have them rolling in the aisles with laughter.

This has been something that Steve and his wife, Ainsley, have been doing since the 1980s, and they haven't stopped.

My connections with Steve and Ainsley go way back. They came to play at my church in Hamilton in 1991 when I was boarding with my pastor, Nick Klinkenberg and his wife Karen and their three boys. My parents had recently moved to the Apirana's hometown of Christchurch to pastor a church.

Turns out that Karen and Ainsley were pals from when they lived in their hometown called 'Australia'. So Steve and Ainsley stayed with the Klinkenbergs when they came to play at our church, and that was how I met them.

Steve found out that I played the blues harmonica and kindly invited me to play a solo on his blues arrangement of the old Sunday School song, 'I Have Decided to Follow Jesus', retitled 'No Turning Back'. To this day, Steve maintains I was 'about 12 years old' but I was actually 17, and a burgeoning musician. To be sharing the stage with *the* Steve Apirana was a real thrill. The church was packed, and during my solo performance he whispered to me to keep going for another 12 bars. Adrenalin kicked in and I don't think I've played as well as that ever since.

Over the years, Steve has occasionally invited me to make a cameo harmonica appearance at the odd Parachute Festival and in 2013, I found myself in a band with him and Ainsley called the Redemption Highway Collective, playing rearranged versions of old gospel tunes and hymns.

I met with Steve at Vision College in Hamilton when I was teaching there, and the interview covered many aspects of his life. But instead of calling himself a pioneer, he would rather give props to other people, especially the late Andy Thompson who managed Butler, Steve's first band.

Come and break bread at Steve's dining table as he shares some stories from his life. Who would've thought that this one-time Santa Claus who had won the hearts of Christian music lovers, once struggled to get his music played on Christian radio?

Brett Wilson: Steve, this book is about musicians who pioneered Christian music in New Zealand, particularly popular music. What do you think about being placed into such a group of musicians?

Steve Apirana: Well, that's hard to answer. The most honest answer is that I was a follower. In the secular circuit I just followed the popular music of the time and when I committed my life to Jesus, I followed the Christian musos of the time i.e. Andraé Crouch, Larry Norman, Barry McGuire etc.

When I became more established as a gospel musician I played mostly blues and the only originality was in my approach and delivery. Hardly the stuff of a pioneer. Plus, I was very influenced by other Kiwis on the circuit like Derek Lind, Stephen Bell-Booth, Guy Wishart etc. I guess we all had our heroes and influences.

BW: Sure, we do. But it was relatively new to play that sort of style of music with a 'Christian' label on it. Would you say Butler was your first real band?

SA: Yeah. The band was put together in 1971, and...

BW: But that wasn't a Christian band, right?

SA: No, but we eventually became Christians – the whole band and our girlfriends and other friends. Not all of them hung in there, but we were all very keen at the beginning. Butler was put together through a drop-in centre the Anglican church was running in Christchurch.

Our manager was the minister's son. In fact, he put the band together. He asked us why we weren't in a band and I said, 'Well, we don't have any gear or anything.' They had gear at that place, and I put it to another minister who was running it if we could go down on Thursday nights and practice.

All the staff were happy because – it wasn't their style of music – but it was *music*. It wasn't just bashing around which they were used to, so it made things a bit more bearable. So we started learning Santana and songs by Jimi Hendrix and stuff by Joe Cocker that we liked. That was 1971.

The minister's son got us together and made us get jobs so that we could save up for some gear. I already had an electric guitar. So we just worked together for about a year before we got a gig. It was very laid-back. We practised once a week, so it was serious enough. But then we started getting gigs at places and getting a name for ourselves.

We played lots of free gigs. It was during the protest era. They [the counterculture] were always protesting about something and they would put on a big thingy where three or four local bands would play to get the people there and talk about their politics.

We were one of the only all-Māori bands at the time in the country and so we were starting to get invitations around the country to play at gigs, Māori gigs. Not only that, but just the novelty of an all-Māori band, we started getting invited to schools and stuff.

BW: Your manager was the minister's son? What's his name?

SA: Andy Thompson. We were influenced by him and his lifestyle and his parents and also the drop-in centre. The place was packed with volunteers who just loved God, loved people and loved to serve. So we got to witness Christianity on a practical level, and also hear about it.

They used to have a Sunday night service specifically for the people who went to the drop-in centre. They would invite people to come in and give their testimonies and talk about Jesus, and everyone would go because they provided free toasted sandwiches and free coffee afterwards. That's where we heard about the Gospel.

At a rehearsal one day, I asked Andy, 'What's the different thing between a Christian and somebody else?' Because he was a real *bad* Christian, man. I mean testimony-wise. He smoked like a train and he swore and he, you know, did all the things we did, and we thought, 'Man. He's not much of a Christian!'

So I asked him, 'Are you really a Christian?' He said, 'Yeah, I am.' I said, 'Well, you do all these things.' 'Yeah I know I do,' he says, 'but God's dealing with me in all that.' He says, 'The thing that makes me a Christian is I have a relationship with Jesus Christ, which is more important to me than anything else, and through that I deal with this other stuff.' And I thought, 'Oh. Are you allowed to do that?' [Laughter]

Because I always thought you had to clean up your act, you see? And he says, 'Well, that's what I do, and I do it every day.' He said, 'The Bible makes no other way. You don't have to do it any other way. You just have to trust God that He's going to do it. And you have to accept the forgiveness, even if you don't feel it.'

BW: Is Andy still around?

SA: No, he died of cancer in 2014. What was it, honey? [Steve asks Ainsley who's walked into the room.]

Ainsley Apirana: Oh, he had throat cancer.

SA: Yeah. He was really great. He was kind of like a mentor to everyone in the band. He was like ten years older than us and he had the wisdom that we needed at the time that kept us on the straight and narrow. He knew nothing about managing a band, but he loved us and took care of us, and all the people in the business around New Zealand that we were getting involved with had a lot of respect for him. They knew he wasn't clued up for the work that he was doing, but he looked after these four young Māori musicians. [Laughter]

BW: Do you think his approach to Christianity – the idea that a *relationship* with God is more important than religion – was quite radical for the time?

Let's Back Up a Bit

SA: Well, it was radical for us, but it just made sense, you know? In our spirit it made sense. I mean it just got something going in us. We started discussing it and we kind of looked at the subject from then on. And while we were doing that, it kind of dawned on us. We thought, 'Yeah, yeah, yeah!' We spent the next few days going, 'Yeah!'

And all the memories you have of hearing things about God, stories at school and things that happened to your relations, those kinds of things came back. Someone prayed for them and they got healed and you're thinking, 'Oh yeah, that's positive thinking!' Actually, the thing that really shocked me, because I'd *never* heard this, was about the Rapture, you know?

BW: Oh, okay!

SA: Andy would say, 'How would you like to be standing there talking to someone and they just disappeared?' And I'd say, 'WHAT?!' [Laughter]

You know? It's kind of like *Star Trek*! He says, 'That's what the Bible says; two people will be at the grindstone or whatever it is, and one will disappear.' And I'm thinking, 'Woah!' And while it may have influenced my decision [to become a Christian], I was already on my way there. But I'd *never* heard that before.

BW: That whole 'End Times' theme was quite big at that time, during the Jesus Movement. It seems like that theme was quite popular both in sermons and in the music. But we wouldn't really hear about it now. At least, I don't hear about it much now.

But back then, it seemed that the big emphasis was, 'Get ready! These are the 'End Times'! Jesus is coming soon! Maybe tomorrow!' And that came up a lot in the music of Larry Norman, Keith Green, and all those guys.

Steve Apirana

SA: Barry McGuire, Second Chapter of Acts.

BW: Yeah! A big anthem for the time was Larry Norman's 'I Wish We'd All Been Ready' which had the memorable refrain,

> There's no time to change your mind / The Son has come and you've been left behind.

A cheery little number.

SA: Ha! But a lot of the songs were like that because that's what was on the minds of the people. But also, that was a more acceptable time for that kind of thing; disappearing... you know, there were movies... *The Last Day* or something...

BW: I remember one called *A Thief in the Night*, which is how I first heard that haunting Larry Norman song. At the time, I had no idea that it was a legit song from a legit album by an artist that was considered to be the father of contemporary Christian music. But that movie scared the living daylights out of me as a kid! It probably assured my salvation for the next decade, as I was too scared to backslide!

SA: Yeah! *A Thief in the Night*! That's what it was.

BW: If the Jesus Movement had a tag-line, do you think it would've been, 'The Jesus Movement: scaring people into heaven since 1971'? [Laughter]

SA: Well, I know what you mean, but it was quite the opposite, actually, Brett. Most of our crew was loved into the Kingdom. There was such an atmosphere of love and acceptance in the air and a sense of relief that we didn't have to earn or be worthy of what God was offering. The Rapture story was the only one I hadn't heard before. It was a shock to hear, but not scary. It actually sounded quite trippy.

BW: Did you get a sense that the Jesus Movement was happening in New Zealand or was that largely an American thing?

SA: No, no. It was all over the place. It was really huge in New Zealand. I read about it in *Time* magazine, and I'd already become a Christian. I'd just made a decision, and then my favourite guitar player, Peter Green, just left Fleetwood Mac to search for God. That was his reason for leaving.

So that was good for me because he was my favourite guitar player. He actually got into Judaism. But the drug trips he took messed with his mind. He refused money. He wanted the band to give all their money away! That kind of influenced me in a way too.

But another influence was the great Māori evangelist, Muri Thompson. He had just come back from the Solomon Islands; they'd been having a revival over there on a real large basis. He was the one who instigated all the Jesus marches in New Zealand in the 1970s.

All the churches got together so it was the beginning of that whole thing, and also the anti-Christian movement. I've got a friend, I was with him the other night, he was part of the big anti-Christian movement. He had this sign saying, 'God is dead. But don't worry, Mary's pregnant again.' [Laughter]

Plus, it was the folk singers like Larry Norman, as you said. He was a big part of the Jesus Movement, his songs especially. And it was the radicalisation of the hippy people and the younger people; their radical ideas of, you know, peace and love and flowers.

So it was a natural progression to go from hippy to Jesus, because that's kind of like moving towards the ultimate love, if you're looking at it as a progression. But with it came all the music from the hippy movement. Not just that, because there were other bands, but they were very clinical and super straight.

In fact, you had to tidy up if you wanted to play and YFC was a big part of that. YFC and Open Air Campaigners were the main people out in the streets. Those were the two main organisations taking the music to the people. It was middle of the road musically speaking. I mean even in the 1970s and 1980s it was a bit tough with Christian radio. You weren't allowed to bend your notes on the guitar.

BW: Someone actually told you that?

SA: Yeah. No bending the notes because it's too modern, it's too, kind of like... Oh, I don't know why. But they said that they won't accept it on Radio Rhema.

BW: Too bluesy? Too dirty? Too rough?

SA: Too sensual. You know what I mean? Too emotional. If there was an anointing, they wanted it all from the Holy Spirit. They didn't want anything, no offerings from the actual human side of it. It was just not clean enough. So when I was playing for some local singer, they would make me do it again but without bending the notes.

BW: Oh, right. You were recording for someone else?

SA: No, I'm recording for the studio. When Rhema used to be in Christchurch. It started in Christchurch and it wasn't any-

Let's Back Up a Bit

where else, so they'd broadcast from there. They would ask me, 'We've got a singer here who needs a backing guitar. Can you come in and play for them?'

BW: Oh. Live on the radio.

SA: Yeah, and recording. Pre-recording. So we'd do it, and they'd say, 'Can you cut that back?' And the pity of it was the guy recording us was a good musician as well, and he was very apologetic about it.

But the leadership would just ring up and say, 'No. Not that.' Because they liked the 1950s stuff, the Bill Gaither Trio, all those types. They had been pushing for gospel radio since the 1950s so you can understand their hesitation towards other kinds of music.

But that was what they loved and that's what ministered to them and all the people their age who also had been supporting that. I don't know what it's like now, but it was like that all of the time for the up-and-coming musicians; the Derek Linds and the Stephen Bell-Booths and the likes. Stephen Bell-Booth was a lot more accepted nationwide because he was a keyboard player and he did worship-type music.

BW: The irony is that Stephen Bell-Booth did sort of bend his notes from a musical point of view. Quite bluesy at times.

SA: Yes! He did all of these kind of weird things on the keyboard, but they stuck it way back in the mix. But he was a sensual musician as well.

But anyway, they didn't want any bending of notes or distortion. They just wanted a clean, 1950s, Shadows sound. The

Shadows were okay. You could do that. A lot of echo and all that kind of thing.

Open Air Campaigners were around, and they were doing Cliff Richard and the Shadows songs from the 1960s. The funny thing about it was I never heard any black music on Christian radio. No black music for a long, long time.

BW: Really? No Andraé Crouch?

SA: I never heard any Andraé Crouch, but they had white versions of his songs. People like Ralph Carmichael doing instrumental versions.

BW: That sounds similar to Pat Boone singing rock & roll songs by African Americans in the 1950s.

SA: Yeah. He did Little Richard songs.

BW: It's like history repeating itself 20 years later.

SA: Well, history just carrying on. The thing about it is that, if you know the reasons why, then you can understand. Black music is very sensual and very physical, which the white people took to be evil. And some of it was.

At this stage of my life, I don't believe that sensual music is evil: I just think it's physical and emotional. But in those days, black was black and white was white and so they wouldn't have any black music. And this was still the case in the 1980s. And you get people like Derek Lind and Guy Wishart and that singer/songwriter genre; people who have so much to say and have got such way of saying it, but it got wiped out.

Let's Back Up a Bit

BW: They're white but would sometimes borrow from the blues. What do you mean it got wiped out?

SA: It never got played. If they will allow that music now, it's too late. It's what Derek always said, talking about him and I, he says, 'We're too young to be cool and too old to be hip,' or whatever it was. So he says, 'Just wait for another cycle to go around and you'll become like B. B. King, who used to be really good!'

But for my stuff they chose one or two songs from an album, the kind of straight sounding ones, and I had quite a lot of straight sounding songs, and they only picked a couple to go on Radio Rhema.

But like most radio stations, they have a target audience and choose their playlists accordingly, and I guess I just wanted them to play all my songs! [Laughter] By the time people like Derek and I were applicable, we were uncool. You had all the Switchfoots and the thingy, you know?

So we went straight from 'not allowed' to 'not good enough now', you know? There wasn't a little bit in the middle. It's like my ministry. I was always going to the youth groups. I'd never get invited to the big churches; I'd always go to the youth groups. And somewhere along the line the youth took over and I was too old. So I got invited to the... Eagles channel... Southern Comfort...

BW: Southern Star [the Rhema Media station for a mature audience, which is now called Star Radio].

SA: Yeah. So I never spent any reasonable amount of time on mainstream radio. And that's happened with Derek. I don't know whether he's ever been accepted. And to most musicians, radio airplay is a badge of merit. At least, I remember saying, 'I'm on Radio Rhema!'

But back in those days you really thought that the radio station was going to help you and your ministry. But they had their border lines and you didn't fit into that so there wasn't a lot of help from the radio stations. Unless we worked with Tearfund and they'd have a little bit of us, a little bit of live stuff. And then there was always the odd bold person who would get you in. Which was really good. Community radio would accept you more than the gospel radio because they don't care.

BW: Do you remember any bold people that got you into Radio Rhema?

SA: Yeah, radio announcers such as Peter Shaw, June Coxhead and Rob Holding. There was a guy that I toured Australia with, Rob Edwards. He was working for David Smallbone in Australia, and then he started working for Radio Rhema over there and then worked for Rhema over here. I have to say that Rhema have been supportive of me, but at that time, it was just a different time. Some people liked me as a person but never agreed with the music.

BW: They were a bit hesitant towards your music?

SA: Hesitant towards the music but not against the person. I can understand. A lot of people in radio can't help but like what they like and so that gets priority. And they've been brought up learning that one thing is good, and one thing is not. It's hard to get rid of that, even if you want to. And because you can't stand the music, it's really hard to make other people listen to it.

I was encouraged by the Pink Family, both by their performances and their verbal encouragement of my music. I guess they kind of understood the tātou tātou e [all of us] thing. You know? The idea of, 'Just go and do it. We know your heart – just go and do it.'

Because whatever's not acceptable will get taken over by what is acceptable. It's that kind of hei aha [never mind] thing. That's a kaumātua [Māori elders] thing that I used to hear a lot; 'Hei aha. Never mind, it doesn't matter. You do what you do.'

A lot of old people used to say that, and I say that a lot now but in English, to my grandchildren. Because you find out in life, everything sorts itself out and the things that aren't acceptable either get drowned out or get you into trouble. Or somewhere along the line it works out.

I found the Pink Family were like that. I never had a lot of experience with them, but I met a lot of them. All their children won a talent quest as the Pink Family. I don't know what [the talent show] was, but it was the biggest thing in the country. And it was because they were trained up like that.

It was evident that they had some really solid Christian upbringing. The Pink Family were involved with Muri Thompson and his wife Ena Thompson. She was an amazing piano player and singer. All from the 1950s era, Bill Gaither and all that, which I have nothing against. I mean I do [Bill Gaither's] 'Something Beautiful'.

BW: Well, I was going to mention that. I remember hearing your version of 'Something Beautiful' on Radio Rhema. I would say if there's one song that you would *have to* sing at a concert, it would be 'Something Beautiful'. It's pretty much your signature song.

SA: Yeah. Exactly. In fact, most of the songs people want me to sing are the ones I never wrote myself! [Laughter] Like 'No Turning Back'. Songs that I've modified.

Steve Apirana

BW: They're very good arrangements.

SA: Yeah. Well, that's the reason why people like them.

BW: But it's interesting that Bill Gaither wrote 'Something Beautiful', considering what you've just been talking about. When you think about it, you were sort of 'blackening' that song. Yet you *did* get radio airplay from it and it became *your* song.

SA: Yeah. Well, you're talking about the 1990s there. So it took a long time for it to come through. But also...

BW: Late '80s. [My cassette of Steve's debut album says it was released in 1989.]

SA: ...it's only a tenth of the actual song. I'm only singing the chorus, and then I sing a chorus of another song.

BW: 'Beauty for Ashes'. Who wrote that one?

SA: I don't know. I think it's just a chorus. It might be from the Scripture in Song book.

I should've known that. #144 in the 'brown book', key of F (one flat, Mum), written by Bob Manzano.

But I used to do it when I was leading worship. [Sings] 'Something beautiful,' and then you sing, 'He gave me...' just to keep everyone singing. I had been singing it like that before I started playing music. I played it slow.

And then I went to a school of evangelism run by Marcus Ardern and every now and then he would say, 'Brother Steve, have you got a song you'd like to sing for us?' I sang that one and he said, 'Yeah, that sounds good!'

That was the first time I sang it in public and people said 'That's great! That's beautiful! Sounds like Joe Cocker!' Who I was very influenced by as a singer. He put out that 'You Are So Beautiful' song and that might have influenced me as well.

BW: Did you record an album with Butler?

SA: We went into the studio in 1973, after the Great Ngaruawahia Music Festival. Just about every band there got a recording contract. But the producer said, 'We've got this new way of recording. We're just going to play all of the rhythm tracks first and then you can overdub the other bits.' And we said, 'Oh, that sounds good.'

So we did it, but we did every song at the same speed. Because you go from one song to the next. You needed to have a 10 or 15-minute break. So all our slow songs were not slow enough. We couldn't hear ourselves in the earphones and I had some terrible guitar issues. I was playing a lot of Wishbone Ash at the time and I was doing all these Wishbone Ash licks in it. When I heard it back, I thought, 'Good grief! I can hear that same lick about 14 times in all the songs!' [Laughter]

So I'm very cringey about it, but I loved the experience of it, but the record company kind of neglected the album. By the time it came out it was 18 months later. We weren't even doing that style of music anymore. But I look upon it, as a Christian, as giving us an opportunity to go and work where God wanted us to be.

With the other guitar player, Matt Warren, we kind of decided to split up because the bass player [Robert Adams] wanted to get his marriage back together again. Because the lifestyle was terrible. So we split up.

The drummer [Hori Sinnott] had gone to Australia. But Matt Warren and I said, 'Well, we're getting really serious with the Lord here. Why don't we just check it out and if there's nothing here, or if it's not good enough for us, we'll get on with our music. We'll just put another band together or get the old boys back together.' And we said, 'Yeah.'

So we used to have meetings together at his house on a Friday night. Keep us from going to the nightclubs.

STEVE MID-SOLO DURING A BUTLER GIG.

It was just a big move of God in our lives. It was just obvious that God was there, and it was obvious that He was concerned with our individual reconciliation with Him and that was more important to Him than anything that we were able to do.

Because we wanted to become rock stars for Jesus, you know? Even as Christians. But He was more interested in getting us prepared for eternity, but also sorting our life out now. So we gave the music thing away for a while.

BW: As a Christian, was it an issue that Butler played secular music?

SA: It was a big issue. It just turned our lives upside down. There was always that clash. On the one hand we had just dedicated our lives to Jesus, and on the other hand we had just entered a realm and a zone where sin is just everywhere.

And all of a sudden, all the temptations that you were not allowed to succumb to where just running at you. The sex, the drugs, the alcohol, that whole life. We were trying to hold off. But this is part of the reason you become a musician; to get all that kind of culture! [Laughter]

So we resisted for a little while, and then you think, 'Oh, what the heck!' And because you tried it you think, 'Well, I didn't get struck by lightning.' Your defences go down and, 'Hello sex, drugs and rock & roll!' So it was always up and down. I mean I had a guitar with a 'Turn to Jesus' sticker on it, you know?

So people didn't mind it, it didn't offend them that I was a Christian. But they'd be looking sideways when they saw me getting stoned or chatting up a young woman, you know? That kind of thing. It was terrible. But having said that, I can only speak for the other guitarist and myself; it weighed heavily on my mind. We had tasted the new wine and everything else was revealed for what it really was: just temptation to keep you out of the Kingdom, or keep you distracted at least, and also to make you a bad witness.

BW: Right. So there was certainly a battle with the rock & roll lifestyle, but what about with the music itself? Did you think, 'I'm a Christian so maybe I should re-look at the songs I'm singing' or was that not an issue?

SA: It wasn't an issue in terms of having a clash, but then I was in the frame of mind where hardly anything was an issue. It's hazy all the time and so you justify what you're doing. But if you listen to the Butler album there's quite a few gospel songs and most of the songs we wrote were from a Christian point of view. So there was a little bit of that whole clashing of the two things. But in the end, we got right out of it. We made a decision, we actually discussed it. We said, 'Let's check out Jesus'.

BW: What came next after Butler?

SA: Butler split up in '77, I think. And then I stopped playing. I was a solo parent. I had two kids from my first marriage and then split up, and I ended up with my kids. But in 1979, I was in a gospel band called Judah.

The reason I was in that band was because Wally Tairakena [drummer] and I were flatting together. Wally said, 'Why don't you come around with me and you can teach me about Jesus?' Because I'd been a Christian about a year more than him, so he thought I was Billy Graham, you know? [Laughter]

He said, 'You come 'round and tell me all about Jesus, man, and you stay at my place and I'll go to work. I'll look after you and your kids. You just look after your kids.' You know? A real generous heart. So I just stayed there almost a year. Just cleaning the house and making sure everything's fine and cooking food and looking after my kids.

Wally had a set of drums out the back; a 12-piece Santana drum-set! For a gospel band! He would come back from band practice and I'd say, 'How's the practice going mate?' He'd say, 'Practice?! All I was doing was ding-ding-tick, ding-ding-tick, ding-ding-tick, ding-ding-tick!' [Laughter]

He said, 'It took me three-quarters of an hour to set my drums up, but they didn't want anything! They just wanted ding-ding-tick, ding-ding-tick!' [Laughter]

The guitarist for Judah was leaving so I said, 'Oh, I'll fill in until you get a real guitarist.' And one of the girls in the band said, 'Oh, that's not much of a commitment!' And I said, 'Nah. You want commitment? Okay. I'll join for good if you like?' So that's it.

I had just said to the Lord, 'I don't care if I never play music anymore because what's more important is our relationship together. Because I have tasted a new wine, and it's good.' So I guess when I look back on it, that was enough for God to say, 'Okay. He's in.' So that was the beginning of me playing gospel music. I was in Judah for about six years, and then left.

BW: What sort of songs did Judah do? Were they originals?

SA: Mostly originals. Everyone in the band, including the drummer, contributed songs. Our bass player, Tony Bayley, wrote most of our songs and wrote amazing choruses. He comes from a family of musicians and his two brothers, Kevin and Colin, they were in pretty well-known bands like Chapta, Rockinghorse, Mi-Sex, and Men at Work, as well being session musicians in Australia.

BW: You call Judah a gospel band. Does that describe the type of music?

SA: No, no. When I say, 'gospel music' I mean 'Christian music'. Judah was more folky-country-semi-worshipy. The songs had real interesting and intellectual structure and chords and it made you want to sing. Everyone was singing together, focused on the Lord.

And in 1977, Jesus was supposed to be coming back. Because it had two sevens in it! He was coming back soon, everyone believed that. But in the end, He didn't come back. So everyone said, 'Oh... let's get married eh? You wanna get married?' 'Yeah, okay!' So they all started pairing off! [Laughter]

Judah's music started moving with the trends at the time. You started getting a lot of younger people who liked the loud punk thing. Wally took over the band after a while and played guitar. He did a lot of reggae and ska and writing stuff like ah... what's that guy's name who sang 'Don't Worry Be Happy'?

BW: Bobby McFerrin.

SA: Yeah. He was writing that kind of funny, silly, talking stuff. But one thing I benefitted from after Judah was going on tour in Australia with Mike and Viv Hibbert in 1979. A couple who led worship music. I just observed how they operated, and I learned to focus less on the performance and more on the spiritual side of things and encouraging people. More ministry rather than performance.

BW: Right. Then later you played secular 1960s covers in the Velvettes. The whole novelty of the band – Blues Brothers type outfits and characters that you adopted – was that your concept?

SA: Yeah. It was a party band. I was brought up in that era where bands got dressed up and did all the moves. The show band thing. It was a rock & roll band playing songs from the 1960s. The philosophy of the Velvettes was, ability: 2 out of 10, attitude: 11 out of 10.

We're going to go around and play as if we're real massive masters but we're going to play real, real terrible. In fact, I had to wear my guitar so low, so I made mistakes and stuff. And we had all of these solos that were really corny.

Let's Back Up a Bit

BW: And you were all Christians?

SA: Yeah.

BW: It might not seem like a big deal now, but in the '80s, secular rock music was considered 'evil' for many Christians, and even *Christian* rock music was seen as a tool for the devil, despite the Christian lyrics. And here you have the Velvettes playing *secular* rock music! I saw you guys when you opened for Petra.

SA: Oh, right!

BW: That was my first ever concert. But anyway, the Velvettes played a lot of '60s songs. You must remember some of the songs?

SA: I remember all of them. [Laughter] We did 'Apache' by the Shadows, with all the moves. We did 'The Rise and Fall of Flingel Bunt' which is another Shadows instrumental.

BW: Wait! What? 'The Rise and Fall of...'

SA: 'The Rise and Fall of Flingel Bunt'. [Steve sings the guitar riff – as if that's going to clear things up for me.]
    I think we did 'Wipe Out'. We did 'With A Girl Like You' by The Troggs [starts singing 'I want to spend my life...'] We did 'Runaway' [by Del Shannon – breaks out into a falsetto 'I wah, wah, wah, wah, wonder...'] I think we might have even done a Beatles song.
    I put the band together because Wally said, 'I'm going to put on a New Year's Eve party for the Māori and Samoan Christians.' Because what would happen is, they would go to

New Year's Eve celebrations in town, have a good time, get drunk, get stoned. Well, they couldn't forgive themselves and for the next six, seven, eight, nine months, they're not going to church anymore. They just get too condemned.

So Wally says, 'Well, I'm going to put a party on for them, so they don't have to go to those celebrations.' He says, 'You reckon we can put a band together for it?' I said, 'Yeah.' And I had this idea of having all these fullas all dressed up, looking cool and over-doing everything.

I got together with [Graham] Flaws because Flaws has some great ideas. He was the bass player and singer. We had another guy called Johnny Mo [on guitar] and he knew all the songs too. So we had Wally, Johnny Mo, Graham Flaws and me.

The New Year's Eve party was a big hit and so someone said, 'Can you play at my 21st in May?' So we already had another gig. And someone rang up and said, 'I believe you've got a rock & roll band?' I said, 'Yeah.'

And they invited us to play at the first Parachute Festival, which was called Mainstage, in Otaki. They got the Steve Apirana Band, the Velvettes, the Graham Flaws Band. They got three acts in one.

BW: Did Kit Grenon replace Johnny Mo?

SA: No. Johnny Mo left, and we had a guy called Don McKenzie, who was playing in a band with Kit. He was in the band for a year and when he left for Melbourne he said, 'Get Kit to play. He'll play anything.' Kit's mum used to make me talk to him because he was a guitar player, playing all the 'wrong' kind of music.

She wanted me to talk some sense into him and 'Be like you, Steve. I want him to be like you.' And I said, 'Yeah, alright.'

Let's Back Up a Bit

So I'm talking to Kit and I look at him and I think, 'He's fine!' He's playing all this Joe Walsh stuff you know? I'm thinking, 'I love that!' [Laughter]

So I never actually told her, but I never said anything to him. I just said, 'No, you're doing alright.' And he had some real neat mates.

BW: So his mum was concerned for his spiritual well-being based on the music he was listening to?

SA: Yeah. He was only about 14 or something. But out of all the bands I've been in, the Velvettes was the most successful. Because no one cared. It was a party band. It was specifically designed to spread joy among the body of Christ.

BW: But you were doing that with secular songs.

SA: Yeah.

BW: Were you ever confronted with people saying, 'Hey, what's all this about?'

SA: Yeah. We were denied gigs because of it.

BW: Oh, Okay. So some people cared.

SA: Yeah. The thing about it is, everything about the Velvettes was wrong. But...

BW: How did you justify it at the time?

SA: I didn't. I just liked it.

BW: What do you mean?

SA: I liked the music, for a start. I liked the attitude of people thinking they're rock stars, and they're not. I liked the attitude of strutting it. The ridiculousness of strutting. I liked that.

BW: But what would you say to people who might say, 'Music should be a tool for evangelism'?

SA: Well, I don't believe that. I used to agree with it. In fact, I went really hard out on it thinking that worship music is the only real music. But I believe music is something to enjoy. I think it can be used for all sorts of things. But basically, to me, it's to express yourself and to enjoy it.

Graham Flaws brought this to my attention. He said, 'Being in the Velvettes has made me realise the most important thing about what we do is for the audience.' He said, 'If they go away being really glad they were there, to me, that justifies what you do.'

There are so many things they [rock music detractors] don't understand about it. And there's so many things the Bible says that can be interpreted in so many different ways, I don't even bother with it. I just do my best and I say, 'Well, let's just go out there and make people happy and do what we can.' And that's what we did and that's what made the Velvettes so successful.

I mean Don McKenzie was such a stickler for doing the right thing. When he first saw us, he said it just blew him away. He said, 'Because you were doing everything wrong! Everything that I believed in, you did it wrong! You're supposed to be humble people and here you are up there saying, "Look at me!"'

But it was bringing out the ridiculousness of it all and so we kind of over-did it to bring that out. We never saw it as a gamble, we just saw it as, 'Let's just have some fun and see if anyone else is willing to have fun.' So we got invited to lots of places just to bring joy. And then the music became really good. [Laughter]

BW: The music from your solo career is quite different to the Velvettes, especially the lyrics. That's not to say that your concerts are not entertaining – they surely are. But if someone only heard your albums, they would miss out on the humorous aspect which is a *huge* part of your gigs (and another conversation in itself). Your songs are quite direct in terms of a Gospel message. In fact, some of them are...

SA: Quite full on, eh?

BW: Well, quoting Scripture. I mean one song is 'Psalm 61'. Did you feel compelled to do that as a solo artist?

SA: Only compelled in terms of that's where my heart was at the time. It just meant so much to me.

BW: You didn't think, 'I'm a Christian and I'm a musician so I *better* get the Gospel message in there'?

SA: No. You know, I became a Christian in 1971 and when I was in Butler, I used to think, 'Oh, I should write some church music.' I thought, 'What am I going to do now as a musician? 'I love Jesus' and that's it?'

But I never felt compelled to do that. In fact, I often try to go the other way a bit more. You know? Make things a bit more cryptic. I like that whole idea. I thought being cryptic was clever, so I thought, 'I want to have a go at that.' Plus, there were some other songwriters around who were really impressing me like

Derek Lind. I mean I'm always impressed with Derek Lind anyway. I loved what Bob Dylan did on *Slow Train Coming*.

BW: That's a pretty direct album in terms of a Gospel message.

SA: Yeah! You get a guy who's the most cryptic person in the world who writes a song about Jesus called 'I Believe in You'. I mean there's nothing cryptic in it at all! For me, that's the benchmark as a Christian songwriter.

He just came and did what was on his heart and that's what I do now. Some songs I get out of the Psalms. A song like 'Born Again' [*This Wretched Man*, 2011] I got from Muri Thompson. He would say, 'You gotta be born again because you were born wrong the first time!' And that stood out to me a lot. But half that song is tongue-in-cheek.

I believe that whatever people get from my songs, God will put it there supernaturally. And I've heard people get certain things from my songs that are not even there! I'm thinking, 'No, that's not right! I didn't even say that!' But that's what they got. But the idea of doing things because it's the Christian thing to do, I mightn't say I never do, but it didn't make an impact on me.

Except for the fact that my ministry is to encourage other Christians and that's the perspective where I write songs from; for people who feel like giving up. Because I was a seasonal Christian for at least ten years. And when I say 'seasonal' I mean three months in, and nine months out.

So those kinds of people I feel for, because I see a lot of them around: 'How you going mate?' 'Oh, I don't think Jesus loves me now mate', 'Yeah well just remember that forgiveness is a big thing. The hardest thing about it is to forgive yourself or accept forgiveness.'

Ainsley writes more about the relationship with Jesus and worship-type songs because that's what's on her heart. But I'm still writing songs for people who are struggling, had a hard time, who want to give up.

If there's any kind of message in my songs it's, 'Keep going. Trust God. Put your life in Jesus' hands.' That's been my testimony for the last 40 or so years. I remember someone asked me, 'What sort of music do you play? Soft evangelism?' And I was a little insulted by that. But then I thought, that can be the name you put on it, but I call it 'indirect'. It's not straight in your face, 'You're going to hell' and stuff like that. Some evangelists will say things like, 'People are going to hell. [Snaps fingers] Now! [Snaps fingers] There's some again! You need to get out there and save them.'

But I'm more like Andy Thompson. He's always been my hero. One of the most flawed people I know, but he just had such a strong relationship with Jesus Christ. It was so important to him and it was so – not naïve – but it was so simple and it was real and it was accessible to a person like me who's struggling with life and doesn't know, and who's not even looking for the answer to life.

BW: You've already mentioned Peter Green and Joe Cocker as musical influences, but if I had to describe your music to someone who's never heard it, I reckon there's a lot of similarities between your music and Eric Clapton's.

SA: Oh, really?

BW: Sometimes an uncanny resemblance. Surely, he's been an influence?

SA: Oh, of course! I never chose Eric Clapton as a hero, but the style he sings and the guitar style he plays that's the style that was cool at the time. I mean, he kind of invented that, he brought that through. Peter Green was my main influence. Emotionally, it moved me probably 99 percent. Eric Clapton would have moved me about 70 percent, as a guitar player. Jimi Hendrix, 80 percent. I like Jimi Hendrix because he was black, I was black, he was outrageous and innovative, and I like all of that but...

BW: But even in the albums you've recorded over the years, I think in many ways, it mirrors the career of Eric Clapton. Because of the different styles of music that you do; sometimes it's bluesy, sometimes it's folky, sometimes it's kind of country. Reggae. Clapton did all of that in quite a polished way, like your music. You've both done straight-up rock or pop music.

SA: Well, even Peter Green was influenced by Eric Clapton, but they were both influenced by the same kind of artists; black Americans. But the thing about Eric Clapton is that he's still current. And that's why I kind of sound like him; we've got the same style of singing, we've got the same style of guitar playing and the same style of writing and stuff.

But I have to say it was not completely intentional; it was more environmental. It just kind of hit me. But I was influenced by the Howard Morrison Quartet. You know, four Māori boys with a guitar on the stage. That was the first band I saw. It's only one guitar but four people creating something together. So ever since then I wanted to be part of a group.

A lot of my ministry has been mostly solo stuff and now we're [he and Ainsley] doing the duo stuff. But most of my influences

Let's Back Up a Bit

AINSLEY & STEVE.

have been from a non-musical point of view. It has to do with how they impressed me as a person more than a musician. Like Barry McGuire. He's my all-time hero.

BW: Is that right?

SA: Yeah. Because you go away from his concerts going, 'Man! God's good to that fulla!' Because he just tells them how good God is to him, you know? I mean he does his songs going blunka-blunka-blunka on the 12-string guitar, and normally he's only got nine strings left and it's out of tune! [Laughter] But he's just told you about this wonderful life he's having.

BW: An incredible storyteller. Which is also a big part of your gigs.

SA: And he doesn't even mention God sometimes! He's talking about dolphins and tea-towels and stuff! [Laughter] But, you know? You go away thinking, 'I want to know that God that is good to Barry. If He's that good to Barry, how come He's not that good to me?' And I go and ask God, you know, 'How come you're good to Barry?' And He says, 'Oh well, there's plenty more where that came from mate!'

BW: Do you think the storytelling and humorous aspect of your gigs came from Barry McGuire or were there other people? Or is that just you?

SA: Well, when I was in Butler, the amount of words you speak on the stage, you'd fit into a small sentence. You know? One line. [Adopts a barely audible mumbled voice] 'The next song is by Jimi Hendrix…' Just let the music speak.

But when I was in the Velvettes I took on a persona and my name became Vini. Vini Velvette. Vindleton Alf Velvette was my full name. Vini for short. And I was him, you know? All the showing off, I just went overboard, and we all did because we had that person to hide behind. It's not really us, but it made me think you can do that!

So when I started doing my own ministry, I took the aim as if you're sitting around a table with a whole lot of people having a meal, and you're just chatting. And so that's the attitude I like to take to the stage. A lot of Māori families are like that. That's how you get to know everybody.

When I was flatting with my Māori friends, we would have a meal together then sit around for two or three hours. Just sitting around, talking, chatting, laughing away, telling each other stories that you've all heard before, but you laugh about them anyway. And all of a sudden, two hours later, you put the jug on again and ah, 'Oh yeah, I might make a bit of toast. Oh, just heat the... lift the...' and you're having another whole meal again!

Because the fellowship has kept you there. And so as much as I can, I go out there and pretend I'm sitting around the table having a meal with these people and whatever comes out at the time, you know? You don't have to think about it. You might see someone that reminds you of something and you think, 'Oh yeah...' But that's where the humour comes in.

The humour definitely came after the Velvettes because it just did the work. It opens people up and you just come alive. Sometimes it doesn't work. Sometimes, like say, in Holland and Czech Republic, you have to drop all the innuendos and Māorisms and stuff because they don't understand and actually, you become a lot more visual.

It starts to become that kind of humour. But it worked for me. I like that whole thing. It's just sharing what you have. Give what you've got, not what you haven't. I think the thing that's helped me the most is to remember that it's not a career; my life doesn't depend on it and even my lifestyle, you know?

I'm not worried about it to earn money. I'm not in it for the money. I'm not in it to be famous. It's to tell people what God's doing in my life. That's it. God has to provide for us. Same with Ainsley and her music and stuff. Of course, we always worry about finances, you know? But that's the reason. It's not a job.

We're not thinking about, 'Oh, we haven't done proper advertising. We need to do something for the young people or the so and so...' Trusting God is the hardest thing and I don't know whether we've got to the stage where we completely trust God. We would love to and, at this stage of our lives, that's who we're relying on for our income, God.

If someone asks us to come, we say, 'Yeah, we'll come!' They say, 'Oh, how much do you charge?', 'Oh, just whatever you've got to offer.' And that's been good. God has provided. It's been pretty hit-and-miss, but He's never let us down. So that's where we are in trusting God in this whole thing. It's a very rewarding thing, but it also brings the wrinkles and grey hair!

BW: And you've been doing that for decades now.

SA: Yeah. Well, I've been doing it since 1989 and Ainsley's just kept everything going for us. She's been doing everything behind the scenes, administration and negotiations. And in the last ten years we've been playing a lot of music together.

BW: Has there been a point where you've had a job at the same time?

SA: No. I was Santa Claus for about two weeks. [Laughter] We were getting paid 50 bucks an hour or something, weren't we? [Asks Ainsley]

Ainsley Apirana: Not that much. But we did get paid well.

SA: You got $25 and I got $25, so...

AA: Oh well, there you go then.

SA: Yeah. Have we had a job? We haven't really, eh?

AA: You can't work and do this at the same time. There's no time to do it. You just have to trust God.

Steve and Ainsley Apirana moved to Noosa in 1992 to be close to Ainsley's family and to be available to pursue international opportunities in ministry.

They have six children and six grandchildren.

Most of their days are spent travelling to places across Australia, New Zealand and different parts of the globe ministering to people through their music and stories.

Over the 30-odd years of touring, they have released six albums between them which are available online and in bookshops on request.

STEPHEN BELL-BOOTH

I wrote my first *real* song after a Stephen Bell-Booth concert in 1990. I was 16 and I basically ripped off a melody he sang, and I memorised it and wrote it later that night. I'm pretty sure his line was 'Don't be afraid'. Mine was 'Look to the sky'. See? Same thing. Please don't tell him.

Stephen Bell-Booth came to my home for an interview just days before his 67th birthday. Similar to the interview with David Garratt, I was a little nervous beforehand because (1) I'd never met him before and (2) his music mattered to a very large audience.

Whenever the writing of this book came up in conversations with people, Stephen Bell-Booth was the most common name they assumed I would be talking to. It's a given. He is a giant in the story of New Zealand Christian music. Not just for his popularity – platinum album sales and crowded venues are evidence of that – but also for the quality of the music and the songwriting.

For Kiwi Christian music, his music was very polished in an age where that was harder to come by because professional recordings were expensive (they still are but technology these days allows you to do it at home and still sound flash).

Sometimes you could tell you were listening to Kiwi music based on the lo-fi production, which might add some charm to

STEPHEN BELL-BOOTH.

a punk band, but that was not the case for a Stephen Bell-Booth album.

I guess I was also a little nervous because I kind of had to address his inactivity as a musician; his last album was released in 1999. It feels a little bit rude to say, 'So... where have you been for 20 years?' I wasn't really trying to cajole him out of his musical retirement, despite some of my questions. I guess I just struggled with the fact that Stephen Bell-Booth made good music that a lot of people had liked and bought.

To see someone, at the top of their game, walk away from that is perhaps not common. Music seems to be one of the few vocations that you don't really need to 'retire' from even when you reach retirement age. At the time of writing, Bob Dylan, Paul McCartney and the Rolling Stones are still getting it done in their mid to late 70s, and they're not just phoning it in either. It's also safe to say they're not doing it to supplement their pension. They don't *need* to keep doing it. They're good at it and they seemingly love it.

Does that mean Stephen Bell-Booth must follow suit? Absolutely not. Stephen Bell-Booth is happy doing what Stephen Bell-Booth does. And since 2005, he has been the CEO for Bell-Booth Ltd, a company that, in his words, 'specialises mainly in the dairy industry .... heifer development and reproduction of adult dairy cows'.

His demeanour was more businessman than musician:

Prompt arrival. Good hygiene. Tidy hair. No visible tattoos. Very direct answers, often answering questions before I'd finished asking them because time is precious, I guess. Or he just wanted to get to the point quickly. Fair enough. Maybe he was always like that even in his muso days.

I also had to grapple with the fact that, for Stephen Bell-Booth, his successes as a musician (there have been many) were behind him and it seemed he would prefer to remain distant from his former life as a musician. He didn't seem to care about his music being unavailable to old and new audiences.

It doesn't mean much to him that he's been awarded New Zealand's most prestigious songwriting award... *twice*. People move on. I get it. But I think his music should be at least available to those who once loved it years ago, and to those who are yet to love it. People should at least have the option to check it out and perhaps see *why* he is a giant in the story of New Zealand Christian music.

Brett Wilson: Have you lived in Palmerston North your whole life?

Stephen Bell-Booth: No. I grew up in Wellington and moved to Palmerston North in '94.

BW: Which coincides with you working with your brother, Mark?

SBB: I went to work for him in '94 and bought him out in 2005.

BW: Has the company always been called Bell-Booth Ltd?

SBB: No, it was originally called R.A. Bell-Booth and Company Ltd. Then it became Bell-Booth Group. It nearly went bankrupt. My brother had another company called Mark Bell-Booth Ltd and I changed it to Bell-Booth Ltd.

The company name, Bell-Booth, goes back to 1960. But we nearly went broke. We sued the government in '87 and it cost us *everything*.

BW: What happened?

SBB: We sued a government department, MAF [Ministry of Agriculture and Forestry], for its role in a TV programme [*Fair Go*] that aired in April 1985. They took issue with one of our products, Maxicrop.

It was one of the longest-running cases in the High Court in New Zealand's history. The Court found a case of negligence against MAF, but we lost our primary tort in that MAF defamed our company.

At the end of the case our business was, for all intents and purposes, destroyed. From a staff of 85, we went down to four employees. In December 1987, after about 20 years in the family business, I went painting houses at age 36.

BW: Wow. So you've done a great job in building the company again. What was your upbringing like?

SBB: I was born in Wellington. I'm one of four kids; one brother and two sisters, I'm the third child. My parents lived in Johnsonville, the same house that I moved out of to get married in 1975.

BW: Was it a Christian upbringing?

SBB: Yes.

BW: What sort of music were you exposed to as a kid?

SBB: Not much. We were Presbyterian and when I was seven years of age, my father and mother said, 'We're not having any of this Lloyd Geering stuff.' [Sir Lloyd Geering was a prominent minister in the Presbyterian Church of Aotearoa New Zealand who faced heresy charges in 1967.] He denied the Virgin Birth and the Resurrection. So we went to the Open Brethren. I was seven and I can remember it.

BW: Who would you say would be some of your musical influences?

SBB: When I was young, I didn't listen to much music because we didn't have a radio. We weren't allowed one.

BW: Was that because it was as seen as too worldly?

SBB: Yeah. My mum came from a very ordinary home. So did Dad. And they decided they would not have a radio or TV. So I had a musically deprived education. I started playing the piano when I was three…

BW: Wow!

SBB: Yeah… I can remember my first chord. That was in my grandfather's house, just down the road. And he said, 'Man! This guy's a talent!' He said to my mum, 'I'll buy you a piano for Stephen.' And he bought one and, thank God, it was a beautiful German piano. Made by a relative of Bach's. It's about 190 years old.

Let's Back Up a Bit

BW: Wow. Was your first chord C?

SBB: No, it was G! I can remember it. I just took to it. Easy!

BW: Was it!? Did you have lessons?

SBB: I went to lessons when I was seven. I hated reading music; I can hardly read a note to this day. I mean when you can play anything when you're three years of age, you can just listen and play it…

BW: You didn't see the point in reading music?

SBB: Oh, it was ridiculous. So I used to cheat my teacher. She'd say, 'Now this is the piece for next week.' I'd say, 'Can you just play it for me?' So she'd do it, I'd go home, never practice it, never look at it, come back next week and play it.

One day at one of the lessons I forgot to ask her how to play it. Went back the following week and I just sat there because I couldn't play it. She hadn't worked out how quick I was. She's just following her syllabus rather than relating to the kid. You know?

BW: So how did your musical career progress? You went on to record albums but you grew up with no radio and weren't exposed to a lot of music. So how did you make the transition from a little kid learning the piano, to eventually writing your own songs and finding your sound?

SBB: Yeah, well… I don't know. I really don't know. I used to play at YFC events and played in church.

BW: So YFC was influential on you?

SBB: Yeah, and I was influential on *it*.

BW: Right.

SBB: I was *good*, so I got a lot of playing jobs and stuff. YFC was influential on me. But by then I was a teenager and I had a radio. I remember buying an Elton John record, the one with 'Your Song' on it. Nina Simone. Mahalia Jackson. I remember watching her on television. It was a Friday night at about 10:30. My mother thought it was terrible.

Because Mum was kind of a trained singer. She had her elocution letters and she could play the piano, but she spoke really well and sang properly, and she thought Mahalia Jackson wasn't singing quite right. And I just thought 'Forget that!' She had *soul*. So she was an influence on me.

BW: I've always thought of you as the New Zealand Christian Elton John. I guess you both sit at a piano, you're both singer/songwriters, there's a similarity in the vocal tone. Is that a fair comparison?

SBB: Could be. I didn't wanna be, but I loved that first album of his. It was a great album. I thought, 'Wow! Who is this guy? He's so good!' I mean he's written lots of good songs but he's not my favourite now.

BW: Did you model your...

SBB: No.

Let's Back Up a Bit

BW: ...sound off anyone?

SBB: No.

BW: Really?

SBB: No. Then I got to know Stevie Wonder's material and then Andraé Crouch. I met Andraé. He and I became friends. He was in New Zealand and I was meant to carry the suitcases for his group because I had a station wagon. But the group got in my car and the president of YFC ended up with the suitcases. I thought, 'Thank you God!'

So I took them to their hotel and on the way we got talking and they said, 'You're a bit of a musician?' And I said, 'Yeah, sure.' Andraé came home and met my mum and played our piano and he became a friend. I used to go over and stay with him in his holiday house. Wonderful man.

BW: Did you play a lot of covers as a burgeoning musician?

SBB: No. Not really.

BW: How did you learn your chops?

SBB: I just got 'em. I just listened. I've got perfect pitch and absolute pitch, which means I can not only identify any note but also *give* you any note. It's a pain in the neck. I'm so glad you haven't got music playing now because, if you did, I would be having to work out every flipping chord of every song *and* have a conversation with you.

So I find music terribly distracting in a business sense or in a conversational sense. I have to work it out and I can't help it, and I'm 67 years of age and it's been with me all of my life. So my chops? I heard stuff, of course, but I developed my own thing. But didn't think about it, just did it, it stuck. I think if you heard me play you'd go, 'Oh, that's Stephen.' There's a pattern there.

BW: For sure. But what about your voice? Vocally, you didn't think you'd like to…

SBB: How do you do that when you've got one voice? I can play funk or jazz or classical, but your voice is your voice. You're stuck with it.

BW: But when I was young I would listen to singers and think, 'I wanna sing like that!' and so I'd try and do what they did and then gradually I kind of put my own thing on it so it wasn't a complete rip-off. You didn't hear some singers and say, 'I wanna sing like that'?

SBB: No. Not at all.

BW: I hear a bit of Chris Rea when you sing.

SBB: Yeah. Love Chris Rea! Love his stuff.

BW: It's a similar vocal style.

SBB: It *is* a similar vocal style. But I didn't know Chris Rea when I did my first album.

BW: But a lot of famous artists talk about wanting to sound like their heroes. I'm gauging your reaction as if that's a bad thing. I think it's a natural thing.

Let's Back Up a Bit

SBB: No. That's where I fall out with a lot of modern worship stuff. It's just so formulaic. You see, David and Dale Garratt, they were just so original. The songs were horrible.

BW: Can I quote you on that? [Laughter]

SBB: They were just corny and ridiculous, and you know what? I still end up singing them. I love them and I draw on them.

BW: They help you memorise Scripture.

SBB: Yep, and they help you in a tight spot. [Sings part of the song 'The Steps of a Good Man'] That is a treasure! It wasn't trying to be cool and it wasn't cool but, oh my goodness, love it! I don't draw on a lot of modern stuff just because there's no heart to it. Now that's generalising. But David and Dale were unique, and I was honoured when they called me up to be part of that album [*Timeless – Music for Meditation* (1992)].

A lot the modern worship music is not my cuppa tea, but I love Brooke Fraser's song 'What a Beautiful Name'. *Beautiful* song. So I'll love it if it melts my heart but some of those songs, they could be sung in a pub. They could be taken any way. It doesn't draw me closer to God.

If I'm singing about God, I want you to know about it, I want God to know about it, I want to bless God, and I want to feel blessed, and I want to be changed. I want to be convicted and I want to be challenged.

BW: I've noticed there's not a lot of information about you online, especially about you as a musician. There would be many New Zealanders who would remember you from when you were active as a musician, but it's interesting that there's not a lot of information online about that.

SBB: Yeah, good.

BW: What do you mean, 'Good'?

SBB: Well, I don't care about publicity. Even in my business. I've got a bunch of guys who work for me and we don't really care too much about publicity. We've got our own thing; we know what we're doing. I've been on television a few times with my job but, no, I've never made a big deal about my music.

BW: I did come across one interview with you conducted by Rhema Media Group's Jon E. Clist and you mentioned that at some point you were playing in America with [CCM legend] Barry McGuire. How did that come about?

SBB: I met Barry through [well-known Kiwi minister and author] Winkie Pratney. Winkie had a friend called Mari and she ended up marrying Barry. He loved my piano playing. He heard me play at YFC one night in Wellington, he was the guest artist, and he sought me out.

BW: Do you remember what year this was?

SBB: Oh... the late '70s? I was at his home when [CCM superstar] Keith Green died. I was staying in his home in Colorado, and whatever day Keith Green died....

BW: In 1982.

Let's Back Up a Bit

SBB: There you go. The phone rang and we all couldn't believe it.

BW: Wow. So Barry McGuire asked you to tour the States with him?

SBB: Yeah. And it was through that tour that I came home and recorded an album. Because I hadn't had great success in New Zealand and I hadn't been out there as a *singer*, but Barry asked me to sing at this concert in the United States. There were a whole bunch of guys there like Joe English [former drummer for Paul McCartney's band, Wings], Phil Keaggy was there [CCM guitar virtuoso], and Barry was the last guy on.

BW: This was at a festival?

SBB: Yeah. Miss America was there; it was this *huge* event. There had been a line-up of guys all night and Barry was the last one on. And *unscheduled*, Barry said, [adopts an American accent] 'I've got this friend from Nu Zealand and he's just written this beauuutiful song. I'd like him to sing it.' Well the promoter had a fit because I wasn't on the bill. [Laughter]

BW: What was the song?

SBB: It's called 'A Christmas Carol'. I recorded it many years later and it's on an album called *Food for the Journey* [1999]. My daughter sings the lead vocal. Have you got that album?

BW: I don't, no.

SBB: Would you like me to send it to you? I've hardly got any left but I've got one and I'll send it to you.

BW: I'd be very grateful, thank you. But that's the other thing about you not being online; your music's not online either.

SBB: I know that.

BW: You're not bothered by that?

SBB: No. I don't care.

BW: Wow. A lot of people who remember your music might care.

SBB: Well, I'm about to put something online. I've just written a new song. It's beautiful.

BW: Great! We'll come back to that after your story in America.

SBB: So I sang the song and people came up to me afterwards, like you wouldn't believe! And *Phil Keaggy* was standing in the queue waiting to talk to me. And I just thought, 'Lord God, this is so hilarious! I can't believe it.' Phil Keaggy came up and I said, 'G'day, I love your music.' He said, 'What was that chord?' [Long pause]

And I went, 'Oh, come on!' And he said, 'No, what was that chord that you played?' And I didn't even know what the chord was.

BW: It wasn't G from when you were three years old?

SBB: No, it wasn't. I thought, 'Phil Keaggy is asking *me* for the chord!' But all these kids came up to me afterwards saying, 'We loved your singing! We loved your song!' And I thought, 'Hmm. Okay...'

Let's Back Up a Bit

And I decided to come back to New Zealand and record an album. I went to Mandrill Studios in Auckland and recorded an album. My father died halfway through it, and that was a bit tough, but Andrew Hagen came on board as the producer and Bruce Lynch came on board as string arranger, and we won an APRA Silver Scroll Award for 'All I Want is You'.

BW: How did you get in touch with these people? I mean, you were an unknown musician and you weren't signed...

SBB: No. There are great communities in the world and you meet people, and I got to recognise that a lot of non-Christian musicians like Bruce Lynch and those guys were so super-talented and they were humble but they were very clever. It was nice to meet some good players.

Someone said to me, 'You need Bruce Lynch on this.' And I said, 'Who's Bruce Lynch?' We met and he listened to my music and agreed to work with me, but his gift to me was a Steely Dan album. I had a Sony Walkman and I remember going back to my hotel and putting it on and I couldn't work out the music, it was just great. And he knew that I needed to be challenged. And that album we recorded, *Letting the People Know*, was pretty cool. It was 1982.

BW: And that was all self-funded, I presume? How was it distributed?

SBB: Yep. Mushroom Records.

BW: Right. So you approached them?

SBB: No. Someone said, '[then head of Mushroom NZ] Mike

Chunn needs to hear this.' So Mike came along and he loved it and he said to the owner of Mushroom, Michael Gudinski, 'I've got a great New Zealand act' and Gudinski said, 'Okay, great. Sign him up.'

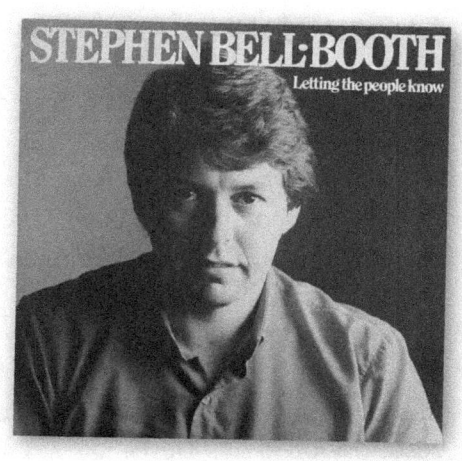

BW: It almost sounds like everything just fell into your lap.

SBB: Yeah, but nothing's easy. It's all hard work. But some connections came.

BW: Was there a drive on your part to really make something happen?

SBB: Well, obviously there was a drive to make an album. Yes, of course. Because I had written some songs.

BW: And you ended up being very well-known in New Zealand, but was it your intention to be well-known, perhaps a bit of a star even?

SBB: ...Yeah... but there's a lot of graft that is needed for that and there wasn't a great outlet for my music because I started at a pub and did some Christian stuff but a lot of people didn't care about what I was doing. And then some Christian places didn't want to hear the stuff I was doing, so I was a little bit of misfit.

Let's Back Up a Bit

BW: How did your parents respond to your music?

SBB: Mum died three years before the album and Dad died during the making of it.

BW: Okay. They may not have heard the album, but you were already a musician and they must have had a sense that you were becoming a musician...

SBB: Yeah, they were pleased but it just wasn't their taste in music. Mum was very conservative. I remember once we did 'Jesu, Joy of Man's Desiring' by Bach, but we jazzed it up for a YFC thing and Mum said, 'I wished the ground would have opened up and swallowed me!' She was so shocked that we jazzed up this beautiful piece. And we thought it was just this huge joke and, of course, I still do to this day but that was how my mum took it.

BW: So being signed to Mushroom, a secular company, were there any big plans either by Mike Chunn or yourself to take your music overseas and really make a go of it?

SBB: No. Mushroom asked me to provide another song for the Australian release. They released the album in 1983 as *Never Look Back*. I wanted to make a go of it, but it just didn't happen. I ended up playing keyboards for different bands and stuff.

BW: Any names worth mentioning?

SBB: I played keyboards for a band called America. Remember them?

BW: Of course! Huge!

SBB: 'Ventura Highway', 'A Horse with No Name'. I did some stuff with Joe English, which was a great thrill because I'd ask him about Paul McCartney and Wings. So I've met a whole bunch of people.

BW: The big album of yours that I remember was *Shelter* (1988). I think that album must have been everywhere at that time. If you were a Christian in New Zealand, you probably had a copy.

SBB: It did well.

BW: Would you have any idea how many copies it sold?

SBB: It went platinum.

BW: Which is 15,000 copies sold in New Zealand. That's impressive. Belated congratulations.

SBB: Thank you.

BW: The album has some guest spots from the likes of Darlene Adair on 'God Will Provide' and Annie Crummer on 'Shelter'. How did those relationships come about?

SBB: Darlene was in Wellington at some point in her life. She wrote a song, she played it and I was a judge at this thing and I met her there.

BW: Fantastic voice, huh?

Let's Back Up a Bit

SBB: Yeah, lovely. I wrote 'God Will Provide' for her and she put it on her album, and I did a different version for *Shelter* and asked her to sing on it. Annie Crummer was in the group When the Cat's Away, so they all sang on the album.

BW: But isn't it just Annie on the title track?

SBB: Yeah, but they're all on the album, except for Margaret Urlich, from memory. And we played 'Shelter' for Her Majesty the Queen in 1990.

BW: You did what now??!!

SBB: It was a Sunday, and Her Majesty was out for the Commonwealth Games and she did three things that day; she attended a church service at the cathedral in Auckland, she came down to Waikato Stud, and then she went to Ferguson Jersey Stud in Otorohanga and I was invited to sing 'Shelter' with When the Cat's Away.

BW: Wow. So thinking about that period, would you say that was the pinnacle of your music career?

SBB: I would think so, yeah.

BW: Are there any highlights... I mean you've already mentioned some highlights. You casually throw it out there that you once played before the Queen...

SBB: Did you not know that?

BW: How would I know that? There's no information about you

as a musician. I don't remember hearing about that at the time. Can you think of any other highlights from any part of your career, not just the *Shelter* era?

SBB: Look, honestly, I've forgotten them. Someone suggested to me that I should write a book but, truly, I've forgotten them.

BW: Okay.

SBB: I've had a good life.

BW: You see, for me as a musician, I'd *want* to remember the sorts of things that you've experienced.

SBB: Well, that was the hardest gig I ever played, playing to Her Majesty. Because she's the Queen! But Dame Catherine Tizard, who was the Governor General at the time, said that the Queen loved it.

BW: Wow. So you must have played in hundreds of churches around the country...

SBB: All around the world. Africa.

BW: You gave up music as a career a long time ago...

SBB: It was a hard game to be a full-time musician in New Zealand and a father of three teenagers. I enjoy commerce, particularly agriculture, but I find the business of music tough. I was offered a job in the rural industry, it had appeal, and it's been enjoyable and rewarding.

Let's Back Up a Bit

BW: Sure. But at the same time, we're talking about someone at the top of their game.

SBB: But I didn't make it out of Christian music. I worked with Rob Winch. He was my biggest collaborator. We did a lot of TV commercials and soundtracks. We had a good hold on the Wellington scene, in terms of music writing.

BW: But considering your achievements as a musician, one might think that you did indeed 'make it' out of Christian music, at least by New Zealand standards. Do you think it's too easy to compare your income, then as a musician, with your income, now as a businessman?

SBB: The income stream was great, or lousy, it all depended on the type and quantity of work available. The income streams included a composite of commercial work including album production, album sales, soundtracks for documentaries, a movie score, jingles, co-writing for child education projects, playing at churches and such like.

As a father of three teenage children I found it economically difficult to sustain the career and made a choice to change.

BW: You mentioned the APRA Silver Scroll Award earlier. Only a handful of Kiwi songwriters have won this award more than once and you're one of them; once for 'All I Want is You' in 1983 and again in 1989 for 'Hand it Over'. What does that mean to you?

SBB: Not much.

BW: Really?

Stephen Bell-Booth

SBB: Nup.

BW: This is New Zealand's most prestigious songwriting award, which you've won twice and puts you alongside the likes of Dave Dobbyn and Lorde. Neil Finn's only won it once...

SBB: Look, I'm grateful that I was nominated, and I won it. And I've been asked to judge different panels and do this and do that, but I'm not interested because my heart's not in it. I really only listen to Christian music now.

STEPHEN IN THE STUDIO.

BW: Why do you think your heart's not in it anymore?

SBB: If I was wanting to critically judge someone in a way that really helps them out, for me to be involved and interested, I'm just not.

BW: Right. But does that carry through to your own music?

SBB: No. I've got a new song coming out soon. It's called 'In Times Like These'. It's a beautiful song and I can't wait for it to be out there.

Let's Back Up a Bit

BW: That's great news! So is this the re-emergence of...

SBB: Nup.

BW: ...Stephen Bell-Booth?

SBB: Nup. Nup. Not at all.

BW: [Laughter] You were very quick to answer that one. Are you too busy?

SBB: I don't have a desire to be musically anything. Because these are times when faith has really been challenged. A lot of people have lost their faith. Jesus said, in the last days, 'When the Son of Man returns, will he find faith on the earth?' It's easy to lose your faith, obviously, because everything's against you.

And there's nothing like the voice of the Lord. And I remember a song that [Andraé's twin sister] Sandra Crouch wrote called 'We Need to Hear from You'. Andraé played it to me and asked me what I thought of it and I just thought, 'How true! We need a word from God.' You think about the times in your life when God has spoken to you and you've just been arrested and you go, 'Oh, that's just what I needed!' One word from Him and it'll fix you. It'll steer you on the right course, it'll reinvigorate you, it'll strengthen you.

BW: I agree. But God has used your music to speak to people in the past. Can't He do it again?

SBB: God can do anything, Brett. He thought it all up. He designed it. And called it into being by the power of his Word. Out of nothing.

I got an email recently from an ex-prison inmate who told me how profoundly God spoke to him and 'straightened his way' through a song I wrote back in 1982, 'All I Want is You'. The email is heart-warming; it put a smile on my face and a pause in my stride, thinking about the way a song can be so impactful.

BW: Do you think you're important to the history of New Zealand Christian music?

SBB: I think I've had a role in it. A small part. I did produce Steve Apirana's first album, which was really lovely. I played keyboards for Brent Chambers and Max Jacobsen's albums and Jules Riding. Yeah, I've had a small part to play.

BW: It's interesting that you mention everyone else's music, but you don't mention your own music. Are you interested in the legacy of Stephen Bell-Booth, the musician?

SBB: No.

BW: You've released a lot of good music which has touched thousands of people, but we have to look back in time to reflect on that...

SBB: One of the reasons I lost the music thing was probably because I thought I'd had my go and I thought I was old and I didn't know if people wanted to hear me any longer. So that's probably why I thought, 'What am I doing?' You know?

BW: Sure. Did you get bitter at all?

SBB: No. Not at all. I've also set music to Psalm 139 and it will be the biggest work I've ever done and it's sounding beautiful. So that's the next job. It's a carry-on from Scripture in Song, except it's the whole Psalm. It's taken years.

BW: So it's going to be a long piece of music.

SBB: It's about 23 minutes and it's one piece of music in six stanzas. So I haven't stopped doing music. I'm writing. I'm looking to work with some really super-talented people who love God and are great communicators, to make these new songs heard further, wider. I feel my assignment is to write the material. It's for others to co-arrange and perform.

I received a copy of *Food for the Journey* in the mail about a week after this interview. Stephen and his wife, Julie, also took me and my wife, Pam, out to the finest restaurant in Hamilton the next time they were in town.

    I am also pleased to see that since this interview, Stephen Bell-Booth, the musician, has embraced social media and posted a live version of a beautiful new song called 'Here'. This will feature on a new album based on Psalm 139, which is slated for release in 2021. He has also released some of his older music online for us all to enjoy.

PHIL JOEL

While Drinkwater only released an EP and one full album, their effect on Christian Kiwi youth was large in the early 1990s. This was mainly through their energetic live shows, which amplified their funk-rock even better than their recordings. If Drinkwater came to your town, you had to be there because a good time would be guaranteed. So that's what a lot of youth did; turned up to their gigs in droves.

Drinkwater was a local Christian band you could proudly show off to your mates who perhaps weren't regular church-goers; a cross between the Red Hot Chili Peppers, Lenny Kravitz, Supergroove and perhaps a teeny bit of Ugly Kid Joe.

The definitive Drinkwater line-up is shown on the *Three Murky Vibes* album cover, pictured later (from left to right): Phil Joel (vocals/guitar), Dean Rush (drums) and Mark Bourgeois (bass).

To get some sort of sense of Phil's personality, consider that in this interview he uses the word 'fun' 11 times and the word 'jump' (and its variants) seven times. Okay, if that doesn't sum him up entirely, then it does an adequate job in describing the music of Drinkwater; fun music you could jump to (and I do recall a lot of punters stage diving and crowd surfing too).

I first saw Phil in action when I was in my late teens. His skill as the ultimate frontman was immediately noticeable, pretty

PHIL JOEL (PHOTO CREDIT: Max tsu).

much to the point where I thought, 'Can you do that in New Zealand? I know you can do that in America. You're *expected* to do that in America. But who does this guy think he is? Jon Bon Jovi? I mean even his hair is rock-star ready!'

Please forgive me, Phil. Sadly, the Tall Poppy Syndrome is a classic Kiwi response when someone else is very good at what they do and perhaps they're not too shy about it: 'Hey bro! Pull your head in! Don't try and be special!' Why should they be shy about it? Humble? Yes. Arrogant? No. But nobody should be ashamed of their talent just because it makes them stand out from the pack.

I think other cultures do better in terms of lifting one another up and giving credit where it's due. Take the Americans, for example. Cue your best American accent: 'Dude, you're freakin' awesome on lead vocals! I totally loved your show!' I can hear that in an American accent more than I can hear it in a Kiwi accent... sadly. The most we can muster up is, 'Shot bro!' And that's if you're lucky.

At least Kiwis can pronounce 'Urry'. That was Phil's original surname, but when he moved to the USA it turned out to be a bit of a mouthful for the Americans. Go on! Try saying 'Urry' in an American accent – it's fun! So to make things easier, his middle name became his surname.

Anyway, you can't be shy if you want to be a rock-star and here was one in the making, right before my eyes. Drinkwater's version of the theme to the kids' TV show *Sesame Street* was a highlight. It contained a snippet of 'The Number Song' from the same show. If you know the words, sing it with me: 'One, two, three, FOUR, FIVE, six, seven, eight, NINE, TEN, eleven, twelve!' Yeah! High fives everybody!

I remember guys around my age playing Drinkwater's version all over the country. It was because of that song, and a few other Drinkwater songs, that budding guitarists all over New Zealand were introduced to Drinkwater's seemingly favourite chord: E7(#9). Just listen to the intro of 'Foxy Lady' by Jimi Hendrix and you won't miss it.

As Phil and I chatted, it turned out we had a few things in common, particularly our love for the Newsboys' demo tape, *He's Coming Back* (1987). This went out of print a *long* time ago and, until recently, it was largely unavailable online.

Let's Back Up a Bit

You had to be at an early Newsboys' show to get it and, thankfully, my brother attended said gig and purchased said tape.

What's kind of cute is that two members from the band signed the tape both with the phrase, 'Rage for Jesus!' ('What did you put? Oh, 'Rage for Jesus!' Yeah, same!') This was back in the day when a gig was a 'rage'. True story.

Another thing Phil and I shared was our slight disappointment when hearing Newsboys' first real album, *Read All About It* (1988). The one thing the demo tape has in common with Drinkwater's music is the sheer energy and, sadly, that was lost on the Newsboys' debut album, in my opinion. So that was it really, for me and the Newsboys. We parted ways.

I have nothing against what they went on to do, but it just sounded like a different band to me, that's all. They certainly had the last laugh, though. The band that originated in Australia went on to become one of the biggest CCM bands this planet has ever seen.

This story takes an interesting twist when Phil Joel Urry became Phil Urry Joel when he was recruited by the Newsboys as their new bass player. Though I had never met Phil, I was as proud as Punch that he went off overseas to become famous in other countries, not just in New Zealand. Admittedly, I was also quite surprised as the music of both bands was a bit different and... Phil doesn't play bass... does he? But I have to say that one of his contributions to the band, 'Entertaining Angels', is their best song ever, in my humble opinion.

Only a few years after I first witnessed Drinkwater, Phil made America his home, playing with the Newsboys, and later doing his own various projects. It's as if New Zealand was never going to be big enough for this energetic guy with the long, curly, blond hair. He would be better off in a place where tall poppies are never too tall.

Phil Joel

THE COVER OF THE DEMO (LEFT) WITH AUTOGRAPHS AND MESSAGES INSIDE (RIGHT).

After a lot of organising with Phil's wife, Heather, I video-called him during a break in recording the first album for his latest band (Zealand Worship) in Nashville ('Music City, USA').

Time has been very kind to both the Joels, as they don't look a day over 25. I also detected a slight American accent on Phil. Fair enough. The dude's now been there for 25 years.

Phil Joel: Happy New Year! [pronounced 'Happy Nu Year!'] So Garry Schäche reached out to me saying that you wanted to do this interview. He's a wealth of knowledge. He was just a

Let's Back Up a Bit

Christian music enthusiast and then he started promoting concerts. He brought the first Newsboys' tour down to New Zealand. So he was promoting a lot of stuff. He promoted Stryper concerts and brought some of that stuff in. He was a good friend who was very encouraging.

Brett Wilson: I've got this thing here… [I show Phil the Newsboy's demo tape mentioned earlier].

PJ: THAT'S IT!!! [Laughter] I LOVE THAT TAPE!

BW: I really love it! There's a lot of energy on there.

PJ: Me too, man! That was Garry. He brought them across and did a whole bunch of shows with them. But that tape! That's great! I think I've got two copies in the basement somewhere here.

BW: They must be collector's items.

PJ: They must be.

BW: My brother went to that gig. Unfortunately, I didn't go. But he got the tape and it's really cool.

PJ: Well, I was waiting for their first American album, *Read All About It*, and I got it. I was actually with Garry Schäche when I bought it. At Shelterbelt Festival outside of Wellington.

Considering Shelterbelt was in Te Puke, Phil either bought it there or near Wellington at Mainstage, the festival that became Parachute.

I remember listening to it going, 'Oh man... Oh, I'm not sure about this.' Because it wasn't the same. You know?

BW: I *do* know what you mean! [Laughter] I just so happened to buy that same album at Shelterbelt.

PJ: It was just really different.

BW: And little did you know then that you would be their bass player in years to come.

PJ: Well, actually, I met Peter Furler [Newsboys' drummer and later lead singer] at that festival. I was 14 years old and I'd just started playing guitar and I saw him at the sound booth. He was watching a band play. He might've been watching Hoi Polloi actually.

And I went up to him and said, 'Hey man, I really love your band!' And he goes, 'Thank you!' And I said, 'One of the reasons I really love your music is because everyone's getting keyboard players now and everything's just full of synthesisers, but not you guys.' And he goes, '...Yeah... we just got a keyboard player.' [Laughter]

BW: A proud moment!

PJ: That was the first time I met Peter Furler! And it wasn't for another six years, when Drinkwater opened for Newsboys.

BW: I might have been at that gig. It was in 1994 at the Mandalay in Auckland.

PJ: Yep. That was it!

Let's Back Up a Bit

DRINKWATER AT THE MANDALAY IN 1994.

BW: Did you know then that Drinkwater was coming to an end and you would be going off to join the Newsboys?

PJ: No, I didn't know I was going to join the Newsboys, but they had the conversation within the band. I heard the stories afterwards. Someone went backstage and said, 'Hey, you guys really need to come out and watch this band.' So they came out and watched and apparently they liked it. So we got talking and I said, 'This is probably one of our last gigs.'

So they knew that I was going to be available. But they didn't really think much of it at that point, I don't think, because it wasn't for another six months that they called me. But it's funny you were there! That's cool!

BW: Before we go any further, could you share about your upbringing particularly to do with music? What were you allowed or not allowed to listen to?

PJ: Right. Um... yeah. My family weren't particularly musical. But we did have, probably like every Kiwi home, a record player. It was actually a gramophone. I remember my mother playing a Cliff Richard record, and I remember this as a four-year-old. It's kinda like my earliest musical reflection. I remember listening to Cliff Richard and thinking, 'Huh! I could *do* this!'

BW: Wow.

PJ: I didn't wanna be a fireman. The idea of singing resonated with me. But other than listening to music it didn't really manifest itself till later on, until I picked up a guitar. But there wasn't a lot of music in my house and it wasn't a real focus for my parents, so I don't think they were really conscious of what us boys were listening to.

I grew up in a family of three [kids]. My older brother started listening to a lot of Led Zeppelin, Pink Floyd, AC/DC, Eagles, a lot of that kinda stuff. Like a lot of kids, their big brothers introduced them to bands, and so I started listening to that.

BW: And you had a Christian upbringing?

PJ: Yeah, a Christian upbringing but, you know, here's the boys in their bedroom down in the basement listening to whatever we wanted to at that point. It was a bit of a free-for-all. But that was the sort of stuff I started listening to, originally because of my older brother. And Queen, of course.

But then I started going to youth group at 13. That was where

Let's Back Up a Bit

I met Garry Schäche, and he started introducing us to Rez and Stryper and that kind of stuff. But my particular favourite, at that time, was the Altar Boys. Do you listen to the Altar Boys?

BW: I haven't heard a lot of their stuff, but I certainly know who you are talking about.

PJ: Man, I love it. My son has just discovered them recently. It's great. It's just really impassioned and very real sounding and raw and they speed up and slow down and their tempos are rough, but it's *impassioned*. And at that same time, around 13 or 14, I was really finding my own faith and this music was sort of the soundtrack to it.

It was just good for me and I knew it; it was *good*. I remember riding my BMX bike around the streets listening to the Altar Boys on my Walkman and it fed my soul. And so guys like Garry Schäche and some others started introducing us to different bands like Undercover and they took us out to different shows.

Hoi Polloi were doing their thing, but it was called Jamboree at the time. It became a little bit of a scene, and I picked up the guitar at the same time and enjoyed playing the guitar. But I kind of had almost two worlds of music going on, you know? I definitely liked a lot of mainstream music, but at the same time I gravitated towards a lot of Christian music that I knew was good for me.

As a teenager, at different points, I didn't want to be healthy and so I'd listen to certain things and I'd switch back and go, 'No, I need to be healthy.' I did a bit of a yo-yo at different points because, especially at that time period in the '80s, certain music definitely represented certain lifestyles.

So there was a bit of a pendulum swing as to what I would listen to but constantly, right down the middle, was always U2.

U2 kind of held the line, you know? They were believers, but they were in the mainstream world and that was a good thing for me.

BW: So your parents weren't really influencing what you were listening to?

PJ: No, well I think it was a new thing for them too. Because they weren't really out buying music. My dad would listen to the radio when he was working on the car out in the garage. So Christian music and contemporary Christian music was a new thing for them. They were conscious of what I was listening to, but they didn't really have much to say about it.

BW: Would you say the Altar Boys were your main musical influence?

PJ: They were a big influence back then. And it's funny – it wasn't until even later on when I moved to the States at 21 years old – I started going way back into the catalogue of Neil Finn, Dave Dobbyn and a lot of the New Zealand forefathers of pop, and I enjoyed that sort of imagery and their poetic lyrics. They're just fantastic poets.

And I began to incorporate that lyrical approach into what the Newsboys did. So it's kind of funny that I didn't really listen to that much New Zealand music... well, then again, that's a lie! [Laughter] My first album I ever bought was by the Mockers. Yeah, Andrew Fagan's pretty amazing.

And of course Jordan Luck from the Exponents. Love that. So yeah, there was a New Zealand element to what I was listening to growing up, which I think carried over here in the US, which helped me out quite a bit.

Let's Back Up a Bit

BW: Was Drinkwater your first band?

PJ: Yes, and at that time we were kind of influenced by, you know, the Red Hot Chili Peppers were a thing and Nirvana were a thing and...

Phil's son calls out his suggestion that Living Colour were a thing.

Yeah! Living Colour!
So we were definitely influenced by that kind of stuff. But we were trying to figure out how to put our faith into Drinkwater's music as well which was kind of an uncomfortable wrestle at times, I think.

Because, even though I listened to different kinds of Christian music from the US predominantly, there was kind of a scene in New Zealand as far as rock music and pop music. A lot of us Christians were in bands, but it was almost like in order to keep working and keep doing shows we... I don't know how to say it. It's not that we were hiding our faith, we were Christians, we were believers – but the songs we were writing weren't necessarily, you know, 'This is how to do life and hopefully if you listen to this song you'll find Jesus.' That wasn't really our goal. Our goal was to make good music, live lifestyles that were honouring to God and just have fun.

BW: Well, I think that was a key aspect to the band, particularly at that time, as far as I'm concerned. That was quite different to Christian bands who came through in the 1980s where the emphasis often seemed to be winning souls first and music second. But the way Drinkwater came across was that the music came first. Is that a fair comment?

PJ: Yeah. Music and have fun. We just loved to jump and we loved our crowds to jump. And that's not exactly a lofty goal but we just liked having people jump when they came to our concerts.

BW: So there was no mission or purpose to the band other than, 'Let's have fun'?

PJ: Yeah. I think we were just enjoying life, and that's still a big part of my personality. I love being alive! I really enjoy my faith and I like music and I think the fun element in music is important. But I would take left-hand turns as well and get serious, dive deep as often as possible. But definitely back then it was 'Fun!'

Although we did have aspirations to take it further than New Zealand, we didn't want to go to Australia. We didn't know anyone in Australia, but we did know of some people in the US. Dave Steunebrink was our main connection there. Steiny! He was in Jamboree that became Hoi Polloi, and he managed Hoi Polloi once they were over here in the States.

He's still here and he manages Tenth Avenue North and Paramore and a number of different bands. He's doing really well with what he does. So we knew him and got in touch with him about coming over to the US, and checking out what this Christian music world looked like and if there was a place for us in it.

But before we got to that place, one of the guys in the band got married and we said, 'You know what? Let's just call it quits and go our own way and do different things.' But we always had an aspiration to be in the States, but we never got there. I finally got there on August 13, 1994.

Let's Back Up a Bit

BW: I first saw Drinkwater at a YFC camp called Ocean Harvest at Opoutere Beach.

PJ: Yes! Marcus Ardern was the guest speaker.

BW: Yeah! That's right! I guess it would've been the end of '91 or '92. I can't remember which one.

PJ: Probably the end of '92.

BW: The song that stood out to me and a lot of others and possibly one of the most memorable songs you guys did was the theme to *Sesame Street*. [Laughter]

PJ: Yeah.

BW: I remember you playing that in a marquee and here was this confident young man on lead vocals with curly blond hair abandoning his position on stage and mixing it up with the crowd.

PJ: That sounds about right. That's funny!

BW: Did you always have a sense that you could be doing this for a living? Here you are over 20 years later still getting it done.

PJ: Yeah, still doing it. I don't know what else I would do. I mean I thought music would obviously be a big part of what I would do. I've been here for over 20 years, but I really feel called to be here, and to be a part of reaching the next generation of youth growing up in the US, and music is still part of it.

Phil Joel

BW: This book is about pioneers of contemporary Christian music in New Zealand. Did you feel then or do you feel now that you were leaders of something new within Christian music in New Zealand? I mean, lyrically, you were talking about chilling out, *Sesame Street* and *Bad Jelly the Witch*.

You were becoming well-known for songs that didn't necessarily have anything to do with Christianity. Musically, it was also different. It wasn't '80s rock, it was fun, funky music. But did you have any sense at all that you were doing something new?

PJ: Ah, I don't think we were try'na pioneer anything. And quite honestly, we weren't the best or most technical musicians. We didn't know much. We *still* don't know much! We only knew a few chords. Mark Bourgeois [bass] started watching Flea [Red Hot Chili Peppers] figuring out how to play slap bass and that became part of our sound. But I don't think we really thought we were going to be pioneering anything.

And at the same time I really appreciated some of the guys around; Derek Lind obviously was fantastic and Steve Apirana, Stephen Bell-Booth, they were doing their thing. The Revs, I loved. The Revs were kinda in a similar vein to us. They were just a lot of fun. So I don't know. I left the country after the band finished and became a Newsboy, so I don't know if we pioneered anything because I wasn't there to clean up the aftermath, you know?

BW: Yeah, but you helped introduce the notion that Christian music could be more than a message or a Scripture or whatever. It could be a song about Bad Jelly if you want. I think that was *new*.

Let's Back Up a Bit

PJ: Right. Right. I don't know if we were particularly conscious of a lot of the things we were doing. We were just going by gut instinct and it seemed to work at the time. Although, I look back now and I think I know a little more of what was going on and why it worked.

I just think we were guys that loved God and loved life and loved music and what you give from the platform is what you get in return, and I think we gave off a vibe. We gave off something that was God-inspired and I think God enjoyed it. [Laughter]

I think He smiled. I think He thought it was goofy and fun and He enjoyed watching people jump up and down and watching me make a fool of myself climbing scaffolding and whatnot. So... [Laughter] ...somehow it worked.

BW: Did you receive any flak for those sorts of things? Did anyone say, 'Hey maybe you should be preaching' or 'Maybe your music should contain a few more Scriptures' or 'Your music doesn't quite reach the 'Jesus per minute quota'? Was any of that a factor?

PJ: No, not really. We never really got any grief for anything. I got into a bit of trouble for jumping off things and climbing on things I shouldn't have climbed on. But no, we never caught any of that 'Your hair's too long. You can't be of the Lord,' or anything like that.

BW: Because that was a factor for a lot of Christian musicians.

PJ: Yeah. I think they paved the way. You know, you talk about pioneers, and I think they broke that ground before we had come onto the scene and so people were okay with us looking a little different. We didn't have to fight those battles.

Phil Joel

BW: Were there any battles that you did have to fight?

PJ: Well, the band went full-time for about a year and a half, so in order to pay the bills we had to play everywhere. You know, we couldn't just play church events or youth group concerts because there weren't enough of those.

So we had to play in pubs and clubs to pay the bills. We caught a little flak at different points because people were a little concerned that we were encouraging kids to come out to the bars and listen to us. And I don't know, quite honestly, looking back, we probably *did* do that!

But I don't remember people in youth groups getting trashed or getting thrown out for under-age drinking or anything. Nothing crazy happened. We knew that we weren't try'na be like evangelists in those situations, but we did have a sense that we knew that our presence, just being there, was going to bring some light into a dark place.

So it wasn't just about getting paid; we did feel like we were on some sort of mission. We didn't exactly know what it was, we were young, but we knew being in those places as believers and being unified and behaving ourselves was going to be a good thing. And I don't know what came of most of those gigs really. There were a couple of times we would play a few different songs that were very spiritual and you'd get some people's gears turning, but that was about it.

BW: So you released an EP of six songs in 1991. I have the cassette right here.

PJ: Yeah. We recorded that in your hometown of Hamilton!

BW: Did you?

PJ: Yep. I can't remember the name of the studio. It was pretty cool. We just came down for one weekend and Mark Davenport, who played drums for us at the time, he organised it. He was the great organiser of the band. And we tracked it, mixed it, mastered it and left with the tapes in hand.

BW: I wonder which studio that would've been?

PJ: It's probably written there on the artwork if you've got it there.

BW: Well, that's the trouble; I don't have the cover, I've just got the cassette.

I suddenly realised Phil probably thought I had illegally dubbed the EP onto a blank tape. I didn't. I borrowed it from a friend (thanks Peter Capes!) and never gave it back. It never came with the artwork. I may have illegally dubbed Joe Satriani's Surfing with the Alien, *but not Drinkwater's EP. Luckily, the interview didn't turn sour...*

Who was in the band at that point? It sounds like you might've had a few changes in the line-up.

PJ: Yeah. We had Mark Davenport on drums, Mark Bourgeois on bass, myself (vocals) and Joseph Stradwick on guitar. That was the original Drinkwater. Then Mark Davenport took a job in the UK and disappeared on us but, collectively, we all had our eye on Dean Rush, who was a great drummer.

He played in a band called Hunting Man and we asked him if he would fill in for as long as he could and he did, but he became a permanent fixture and really began to manage the band.

BW: And Joseph left at some point?

PJ: Yeah, because we wanted to go full-time and Joseph still had one year of college learning to become a civil engineer, I think, so he couldn't do it. So the guys said, 'Phil you just need to pick up the guitar and we'll run it as a three-piece.' And so we did. Which, you know, I'm a rough guitarist at the best of times so…

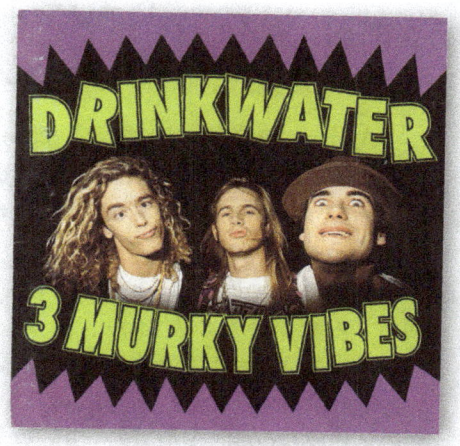

BW: I don't know about that.

PJ: Ha! I just smile my way through it.

BW: What about Joe Hardy? I remember him hanging out in YFC circles in Hamilton for a while.

PJ: Yeah, he was a part of the band after Joe Stradwick left. He came on board and played for a little while. I don't know why he left. Everyone loved Joe Hardy because he's just a lovely guy, but I think he left to take a job or do something else. So we decided, at some point, the easiest thing to do was just to become a three-piece. Less mouths to feed! [Laughter]

BW: The album *Three Murky Vibes* was released in 1993 and on the CD cover it says Fetch Records. Were you signed with a label called Fetch Records?

PJ: No, we made that up. [Laughter] No, we remained independent. We approached all of the labels in town but none of them were interested in us.

BW: Wow, that's interesting because I remember a documentary on Drinkwater, I think it was on TV3. For a band that, supposedly, no one was interested in, how did that come about?

PJ: Ah, I don't know. I think the woman that directed it saw us playing at a pub downtown in Auckland, and there were a few different bands that were around at the time that she was deciding on who to do the documentary on, and for some reason she picked us. I guess she thought we were the most interesting, or crazy or... I don't know.

BW: Sadly, that doco does not exist online. I'd love to see that again...

PJ: Woo hoo! Can't say I'm sad. [Laughter]

BW: Just going back to the topic of lyrics. We've mentioned some of the lighter aspects of your songs such as 'Chill Out [Brussel Sprout]' which, by the way, was delivered in that guttural voice which was always a highlight with your singing. But at the same time, there were songs from the EP and the album such as 'Who Are You?' and 'Hey Lady'. They come to mind for their deeper lyrical themes.

PJ: Yeah. We tried. [Laughter] I love 'Who Are You?' That was a great little song. That was the one I was mentioning early on that we'd play in different bar situations where you'd see people going, 'What is this? This isn't necessarily a love song. What is this about?' You know? That was kinda fun getting to play that.

Phil Joel

BW: Do you want to talk about the lyrics to 'Hey Lady' at all?

Just to give you, dear reader, a sense of the delicate area I'd just dived into with this question, consider that it took 15 seconds for Phil to answer. That's a long pause when you're talking to someone. I knew it was going to be a sensitive issue, but I wasn't prepared for the following response:

PJ: Ha! Ah, yeah, let me think... umm... yeah... well, nah, maybe not.

BW: That's all good.

Quickly moving on! I muster up the courage to bring up the issue again later, so keep reading.

When did you start noticing a buzz surrounding Drinkwater? Was there a moment where you thought, 'Oh my goodness! This could turn into something quite huge!'

PJ: Yeah, I remember walking down Queen Street [Auckland city's main street] at one point and hearing someone yell, 'Drinkwater!!!' from across the street. I turned around and there was a bunch of teenagers kinda yelling and screaming and I thought, 'What? Oh yeah! That's the name of the band I'm in! Wow! Okay.'

And I sort of gave them a little wave and thought, 'Oh... I guess people are starting to like what we do. This is getting interesting.' I don't like using the word 'fans' but, you know, the people that would come out to our shows, they were always pretty energetic and pretty into it. They were ready to go crazy so it was always...

Let's Back Up a Bit

BW: I think 'fans' is appropriate. I remember a group of people in Hamilton who were just kind of fanatics, really.

PJ: A little fanatical. Yeah, so maybe that's the appropriate use of the word.

BW: So in terms of mainstream success, I remember hearing 'Don't Look Now' on the Rock radio station. Was that played on other stations?

PJ: Yeah, it was. It was played all over the country for a while and to whatever degree of success, I'm not sure. It didn't become a number one hit but it was nice, and New Zealand radio was definitely quite receptive.

They didn't really care if you were Christian or not; that wasn't an issue. It was more about whether the music was good or not and if it was going to fit their format and serve their listeners, which that song did, so they gladly played it.

In the US it's a little different. They wanna know who you are and where you come from and what your category is, and which box to put you in. But back then, mainstream radio was just looking for good songs and were open to playing New Zealand music at the time and I think they still are, which is good.

BW: [Takes a deep breath] I don't want to push this, but I think about this song 'Hey Lady' that you don't want to talk about. I just find it interesting that you don't want to talk about it, but there it is on the album for everyone to hear...

PJ: [In an interrogating manner] What d'ya know about it?

BW: Well, I heard that it was about your adoption. I think the lyrics aren't overly ambiguous. But that was a heavy song compared to most of the others on the album. Why are you hesitant to talk about it?

PJ: I think it's okay to talk about it. I just like to try and be respectful to my parents in New Zealand as much as I can because they're such wonderful people and such wonderful parents.

But the song was directed towards my birth mother whom at that point I'd never met, and I just wanted to thank her for my existence. For letting me *be*.

And I don't know what the abortion laws were in New Zealand at that time, but the abortion laws had changed over here in the US, and so a lot of those social movements or political movements happened at similar time periods, if not before. New Zealand is certainly a forerunner in becoming a liberal country.

Maybe the abortion laws were already on the cards in New Zealand where it may have been legal, I don't know. Either way I just wanted to write a song that thanked her for following through and having me and going through with the tough decision to put me up for adoption, which was the best thing that could've happened.

BW: Wow. Did she ever hear that song?

PJ: I think she did. I think it made her cry from what I recall. Yes. She is a really great lady. She lives in Perth now and we're in contact. When I wrote the song I didn't think I'd ever really get to meet her. I just sort of hoped that maybe somehow she'd hear the song. So she did.

Let's Back Up a Bit

BW: Thank you. We mentioned Drinkwater opening for the Newsboys in '94. Was that your final gig as Drinkwater?

PJ: I think it was. If not the final one, it was one of them. We may have had to do a couple more to pay off some bills or something, but that was very near the end of the Drinkwater era for sure.

BW: So you were coming to an end before the invitation came to join the Newsboys?

PJ: Yeah. Oh yeah. They knew that Drinkwater was finishing. It was a conversation we had that night there at the Mandalay. And somehow the manager put my name and face on the hard drive back in his brain and got in touch with me. Three o'clock in the morning, Friday morning, six months later.

BW: What was your initial reaction to that invitation?

PJ: Ah, the funny thing was I had sold everything. I was sleeping on a friend's couch in Mt. Eden in his single bedroom flat. I got a passport and a six-month visa for the US and I was gearing up to come and visit the US and find out what was going on in the music scene over here, and I felt that was what the Lord wanted me to do and where He wanted me to be.

Then the phone rang at three o'clock in the morning, and I thought, 'Oh! This is why I'm ready to go!' You know? They said, 'Our bass player has left, and we wondered if you could be in Los Angeles on Sunday?' And they were calling me on the Friday morning. I said, 'Let me call you back.'

I spoke to my dad and he was just like, 'Yes! This is it! This is what you've been working toward.' So I got a plane ticket and jumped on an aeroplane. I think the Lord had been preparing my heart, you know, through Drinkwater and through some of the different experiences at home, to be doing what I've been doing for over 20 years here.

BW: Your tenure with the Newsboys also coincided with the group's rise in commercial success. Do you think that being a New Zealander had any bearing on handling commercial success in America?

PJ: Well, I think sometimes ignorance is bliss, you know? It's funny; I don't think I even knew the magnitude of what was going on when it was going on. I just enjoyed it and somehow, as New Zealanders, we can sort of roll with the punches and we can find ourselves in crazy situations and manage to keep a level head, you know? And maybe it comes from living under a Tall Poppy Syndrome; I don't know.

But it wasn't long before we were selling gold records [500,000 copies sold in the US] and we were going to the Grammys and doing all that sort of stuff. It was pretty exciting but it was also... all of that stuff, I just kinda... I think being a New Zealander and the way in which we've all been raised, somehow gives us a pretty good perspective on a lot of that stuff where it doesn't really hold a lot of allure, at least it hasn't for me.

It's fun stuff, but the most exciting thing for me is seeing the lights come on for kids when they have an encounter with God through the music or through something that is being shared about a song. That's the most exciting thing because it's eternal, you know? I've enjoyed lots of little moments but when you see those moments turn into a movement in people's lives, that's a big deal.

Let's Back Up a Bit

BW: That leads on to my next question about a particular moment in your career where you stopped and thought, 'Wow! Here I am. This guy from Auckland living the dream making music in a successful rock band!' Is there one particular moment?

PJ: Ha! I don't know... I have some different categories for some of those moments. You know, we had our own plane for a number of years there so...

BW: Wow!

PJ: Flying in your own plane to concerts and flying home and tucking up in your bed by two o'clock in the morning, that was always a pretty amazing thing to be doing and I realised it at the time. I thought, 'This is pretty special. This is a gift and I should enjoy it.' So I gobbled up every moment, you know?

There were other ministry moments which I think will be more enduring in my memory, such as being in front of 40,000 Muslims in Morocco, playing in front of them and seeing the Spirit of God fall on people in ways that I still can't quite understand.

So finding ourselves in some of those really interesting situations in strange countries and singing about the Truth and singing about the Gospel to people who don't even understand the language and watching God move, some of those moments I would deem the most successful moments.

BW: The rise in success of the Newsboys also coincided with the band's working relationship with the producer and co-writer, Steve Taylor. He was already famous for his own CCM career, which was deemed controversial by some at the time.

Musically, he was similar to David Bowie or Talking Heads

and lyrically, he was an expert at critiquing Christian culture and I think he was ahead of his time and therefore slightly misunderstood by some. What was it like working with him?

PJ: Well, I learned *a lot* from Steve Taylor about how he would turn phrases and how he would hear things and how he would see things lyrically and how he would want to twist phrases and twist people's brains a little bit. [Laughter] Which was fun. It allowed me to think a little bit differently.

We'd go out and have breakfast and I would pick his brains on stuff and ask him questions on how he would approach things. He was, and still is, a lot more of a sensible, calculated, deliberate character than maybe people used to think.

They thought he was just this wacky, wild, avant-garde artist and, yes, those things were true, but he's very super-intelligent and highly calculated in the way he operates and in the way he approaches his lyrics. So I learned a lot from him, but he wasn't this crazy kind of bouncing off the walls kind of a guy in the studio. He was very deliberate in his approach and so it was good. It helped me.

BW: Did he make any suggestions that seemed quite radical?

PJ: No. No. He was very affirming of me because we would write these songs and there were a few songs that didn't have lyrics and I thought, 'Well, I'll give it a shot.' So I'd come back the next day with a sheet of paper and say, 'Hey, what do you think guys?'

I didn't really understand that that was probably not what you're meant to do [laughter] because Steve was writing most of the lyrics. But I thought, 'Hey, I'm in the band!' You know? 'Can't I write some lyrics?' So I did, and the band and Steve were pleasantly surprised.

Steve would tweak them a little bit and show me a couple of things on how I could improve the next time around, or maybe a different way of approaching it, or a different way of seeing things. So I learned quite a lot and he was very affirming and very encouraging which was really cool.

He wasn't threatened by some young kid coming along trying to move in on his turf. I wasn't. I just thought I was in the band and we were supposed to write lyrics and work on songs, you know? That was before I understood there was money involved! [Laughter]

BW: Speaking of other people that you came into contact with; there was the former CCM artist, Katy Hudson, who later changed her name to Katy Perry. It's quite fascinating that you were, and perhaps still are, buddies with someone who ascended to the throne of...

PJ: Popdom.

BW: Yeah! She's one of the pop princesses. How did you know her and what was your reaction to her meteoric rise to super-stardom?

PJ: She used to open up for me on my solo tours. I think that was the first touring she did. She was really young and had this other girl with her who was kind of there to try and look after her and keep her on the straight and narrow. [Laughter] She was a lot of fun and really wacky. Almost too wacky for the Christian world, I think.

When she did hit that pop icon status I just kind of thought, 'Huh. There she goes.' I guess I should have seen that coming, but I didn't. But when it did happen I wasn't surprised. I was surprised and slightly baffled by her choice of lyrical content, especially for her first single ['I Kissed a Girl'].

I've had a lot of people calling asking me to comment on what she's doing and whether I think it's good or bad, or trying to poke and prod around and see if they can get some sort of provocative Christian statement, you know? But I won't really respond to most of that. She's doing her thing, I'm doing my thing and the two are very different! [Laughter]

BW: Coming from Drinkwater into the Newsboys, did you have to acclimatise yourself to a softer or more polished form of music?

PJ: Yes. I had to practise! [Laughter] Yeah, I did! Every night after a show we would beat each other up, me in particular. I would get beat up.

They would say, 'Hey, you messed that chorus up! You were singing flat on that harmony! You need to up your game!' You know? So it was good. This little New Zealand boy that didn't really practise a whole lot, I was just used to winging it and flying by the seat of my pants.

At this point, you're in front of thousands of people every night. You can't bumble your way through it: you need to know your business. So that was a good thing for me.

BW: I guess you would've felt more pressure than anyone else, being on an instrument that's not necessarily your strength. I've heard your story about not really being a bass player, and your audition for the Newsboys wasn't going well until you started using a pick.

PJ: Yeah, there was definitely a little pressure there. But the guitar pick, honestly – because I played guitar quite aggressively in Drinkwater – playing the bass with a guitar pick made it a little more aggressive sounding. But it worked and it still does. It works in a big context – that percussive bass sound with a solid kick drum. It became a big part of the Newsboys' sound at that time. It was fun to be a part of re-shaping the sound of the band. It wasn't my plan, but it just happened that way.

BW: There's a noticeable difference between the music of Drinkwater and the Newsboys. I mentioned before your guttural vocal delivery, which I don't think ever surfaced in the Newsboys' catalogue, perhaps it has a few times on your solo records. But have you had any surprised reactions from Newsboys fans hearing you sing like you did with Drinkwater for the first time?

PJ: Oh yeah. Well, when I first played some Drinkwater for my wife, then my girlfriend I guess, she thought it was crazy. She thought, 'What is this Drinkwater?! Crazy stuff!' She thought I'd lost my mind.

Heather chimes in from another room saying she thought it was 'hot'.

BW: But that vocal delivery has come out a few times in your solo career like in your song 'Shout' from *The New Normal* (2008).

PJ: Yeah! I was just thinking about that song when you were mentioning it. Yeah, it's come out in a few spots. The US generally, across the board, is a lot more conservative in their music consumption. Especially churched America.
 They're definitely a little more conservative and so there's

only so far I feel that I can push that envelope. Which, some would say, 'Hey! You're selling out.' But I would say, 'No, we're here to serve.' You know? So the guttural Drinkwater vocal doesn't appear too much these days, but it's probably because my vocal cords aren't up to it like they used to be.

BW: Let's talk about why you left the Newsboys.

PJ: Well, it was only five weeks after I joined the Newsboys in 1994 that I met my wife. So my family and friends back in New Zealand, they just thought I was crazy. They just thought I must've decided to marry the first girl I met in America to get a Green Card or something like that, you know? But that was very far from the truth.

It was just that the Lord had her there and for me to meet her nice and early on in my journey was a gift. So we got married about a year and a half later, and about five years after being married we had kids and, you know, you kinda grow up and you change. My faith grew a lot too and is hopefully continuing to grow and I really began to long for more 'hands on' ministry.

At that point, when I left the band, you know – we had the plane and we'd fly in and do our thing and then fly home again – but we didn't really have a lot of contact with people. It was pretty exciting and a great job, but I wanted to grow and stretch my ministry legs a little more and also I wanted to be home with my family more. When you're in a big touring machine like the Newsboys was at that point... we were on the road for over 200 days a year, so that gets a little tiresome.

I wanted – and still do – to be the husband I'm meant to be and the father I'm meant to be, and I can't be that if I'm gone. That's my number one priority in life; to minister to the Lord and minister to my family and love them.

Let's Back Up a Bit

So there were different roads that led to that decision, and off I went and began speaking a lot more. People were inviting me to speak and share this message that we called the deliberatePeople message, about seeking God on a daily basis. Just a very simple message that would encourage people to get up in the mornings and open up their Bibles, open up their hearts and meet with God and do this consistently, and watch what happens.

Start having that relationship with Him. Nurturing it and tuning our ears with the voice of God. And so that's *still* a very big part of the message that I bring when I minister. Whether I go out with an acoustic guitar and do a solo show, or whether I'm out with Zealand Worship and doing what we do, that's still a big part of our presentation; to encourage people to continue to seek God.

We've been talking about a lot of great ministry moments, but it's the movement of God that I want to see and that gets me excited. When people get a hold of who God is and God's heart for them and when they really embrace that and start to walk in it, *that* gets me excited. More than standing on stage in front of thousands of people and having people cheer and sing along with your songs.

That lasts for a little while, but you know, when people really catch it and understand that God is *for* them, and God has a relationship in store for them, that is beyond exciting. When they catch a hold of that, I can give my life to that. I can give my life to seeing that happen and being a part of delivering that message.

BW: So even though you were in a band that had its own plane and was selling hundreds of thousands of records, it was an easy decision to leave the Newsboys?

PJ: Yeah. It was easy on one hand because as the Lord guides, He provides. I've learned that over the years, time and time again. But at the same time, you're giving up something that, in man's eyes, is very successful and very prestigious and what a lot of people aspire to; to be known and seen.

We live in a very media-centric, celebrity-driven world. It was tough for a lot of people to understand why I would step away from that. But not for me. It wasn't hard. It was pretty simple and it's been really great since! You know, I still get to do what I get to do!

I'm still in front of a lot of people, we're still touring and I get to make music and get to minister and get to be with my family and so ah... man! If God's leading you to do something, you better do it! Because it's going to lead to good things. You're a fool if you don't.

BW: You've started a band called Zealand Worship, which appears to wave the New Zealand flag, considering the band name.

PJ: Ah huh. But it's more than just a tip of the hat to the 'Motherland'. I want to see people zealous for the land. I want to see people get excited about who God is and what He has in store for them.

You know, I was on a plane one day flying home and thinking about names for the band and 'Zealand' was one of those things that just popped into my head and I was like, 'What?!' It's like it was under my nose the whole time, you know?

Obviously it's not 'New Zealand' but 'Zealand'... yeah! Helping people become zealous and excited about what God has in store for them. That's what the band's about and that's our mission. So voilà! Zealand Worship.

Let's Back Up a Bit

BW: Your identity as a musician has obviously changed over the years and through the various facets of your career; Drinkwater, the Newsboys, your solo records, deliberateKids, and now Zealand Worship.

There seems to be a trend over the last few decades where more and more Christian musicians are releasing worship albums. You've already mentioned people who incorrectly say you've sold out, but what would your response be to people who say that this trend is due to worship music selling well?

PJ: Yeah. Well, um...

BW: Someone might say that you started off being similar to Anthony Kiedis from the Red Hot Chili Peppers. Imagine him doing, like, a Bryan Adams love songs album or something like that.

PJ: Yeah. Although, you know, I think if I'm completely honest, the record label wanted me to put 'Worship' after 'Zealand' and I just wanted to call the band Zealand.

BW: That's interesting.

PJ: But I wanted it to have more of a worship emphasis in that I wanted people to sing these songs and make these declarations. You know, if you listen to the music that Zealand's making it's nothing like, you know, Chris Tomlin or that kind of thing. It's still its own thing, but it is designed for people to sing and for it to resonate with their hearts and hopefully embed Truth into their brains, into their souls, you know?

I can't speak as to why that's become a trend in the last little while; I don't really know. It just is what it is. People like worship music at the moment, which is a good thing, I guess. I don't know, man. It's a weird one to answer because I feel like, 'Oh man! I know me and I know my motive and I know why I'm doing what I'm doing...'

And I've felt at different points, 'Oh, what are you doing? Are you selling out, or are you doing something to try and sell records?' And that couldn't be further from the truth. I don't... what? Hang on a second... [A discussion with Heather ensues.]

Right. That's a good point. Heather's making the point that for me, I felt that the CCM world is definitely about, 'Hey, let's talk about me' kind of thing and it's a little bit more about the artist. Whereas worship music is definitely seen as being more ministry driven, and less about the *deliverer* of the message, and more about what is being *delivered*.

So there's more of a ministry focus in the music in what people consider to be 'worship'. So in some ways, to adopt that 'worship' tag to what it is that I do, I'm okay with that because it changes the emphasis. It's saying, 'Hey, this isn't about Phil. This isn't even about this band. This is about God getting into my heart and my head, and that's what I need.' It's a big question Brett – I'm not sure if I'm answering it very well.

BW: I think that's a great answer. At the same time though, you're a musician who started off in quite a different style. So do you have moments where you just want to use that guttural voice and rock out a bit?

PJ: Yeah, and you know, deliberateKids scratched that itch a little bit too. I could've stayed making music as a solo artist, but I felt that the emphasis on the artist becomes too great. I don't like that. I don't really want people looking at me and having T-shirts with my name on it. I'd rather be making music that ministers under a band name, and that's what we've been doing. The band developed through our little ministry unit doing a bunch of youth conferences and that's kinda how it came about.

BW: In the space of two decades, you've achieved success through many facets of your career. Do you think about those humble days of being in New Zealand, and being in Drinkwater?

PJ: I do from time to time. It was a really great time in my life and was a really fantastic training ground and springboard into what I've been doing for the last 20-something years and I look back on it with great fondness.

BW: And you still love to jump.

PJ: I still love to jump. [Laughter]

Phil and Heather Joel live in Franklin, Tennessee with their two kids, three dogs and four chickens. When Phil is not on tour with Newsboys United (a combined line-up of past and present Newsboys' members) he can be found either in his garden or in his home studio working on music for his latest solo album.

HOI POLLOI

Attending Shelterbelt Music Festival was a huge moment in my life. The inaugural event (it was only held twice) was located on a farm somewhere near Te Puke when 1989 crossed over to 1990.

I had just turned 16 and pitched a tent for the weekend with friends from church.

This was prior to Parachute Music Festival becoming the annual go-to event for a lot of Kiwi Christians. The headline act at Shelterbelt was none other than Rez Band, so I was pretty excited to see one of my favourite bands live and in particular the frontman, Glenn Kaiser, who was probably my biggest hero at that point in my life.

My very first band, Deafening Whispers had sent a demo tape to the organisers hoping it would be our big chance to play before a large crowd. Heck, before *any* crowd! We never heard back.

Fair enough. We were as good as our band name... terrible. The thought of including a bad cover of a song by Rez Band on our application to play at a festival featuring Rez Band is embarrassing to say the least! I've since sought counselling and have moved on. Sort of...

Needless to say, I was exposed to many Christian Kiwi bands at Shelterbelt; Ezra stood out for their flamboyant guitar

HOI POLLOI PRESS KIT PHOTO. FROM LEFT: JENNY HORST (NEE GULLEN), ANDREW HORST, JOZSEF FITYUS & DAVE BALL.

work (props to any band that can cover Van Halen's 'Jump'). P.D. Corp introduced me to jangle-indie-pop and a new obsession began with that group's frontman, Jono Jack. (I ended up buying his guitar a few years later.) Other names that come to

Hoi Polloi

mind include Real Time, Charisma, the Yahoos (Glenn Kaiser thought that was a 'crazy' name. Yes, I spoke to my hero!), the Revs and the subject of this chapter, Hoi Polloi.

I wish I could remember more band names (apologies if you played there and I haven't called out your name). I also wish someone would formally document that festival, online or elsewhere, before the memory of Shelterbelt fades altogether.

I do remember a couple of MCs who compered in between bands who I thought were a great comedy duo. I found out much later they were Scotty Pearson (later the drummer for famous rock group, Elemeno P) and Marcus Crane (Tereora Crane these days).

It turns out that playing at Shelterbelt was a big moment for Hoi Polloi, as Glenn – who was obviously so impressed by the band – invited them to play at a much larger festival in his hometown of Chicago, called Cornerstone Festival. I must've been impressed with them too because I bought their T-shirt, though I can't really remember their set. Maybe I just liked the T-shirt.

I do remember seeing other Hoi Polloi shows later though, and, in my opinion, their professionalism was like no other in the local Christian scene at the time. I reckon Glenn must've felt the same way. Plus, they had good songs.

For some reason, everyone in my circle knew the lead singer's name was Jenny Gullen. Like most singers in bands, she was certainly the focal point and in my opinion she carries a voice that, along with Darlene Adair, is one of the most unique voices in Christian music in New Zealand.

Sadly, no one in my circle knew the names of the other band members. So this is a few decades late, but apologies to Jenny's husband and Hoi Polloi bass player, Andrew Horst, Hoi Polloi guitarist Dave Ball, and Hoi Polloi drummer Jozsef Fityus. Dave and Jozsef were later replaced by American guitarist, Troy Daugherty and the aforementioned world-famous-in-New Zealand drummer, Scotty Pearson, followed by Matt McGuyer from the US.

The band's six-month jaunt to the USA turned into five years. I don't recall any other Christian band leaving New Zealand to make a real go of it internationally, before Hoi Polloi. In fact, how many *secular* Kiwi bands were doing that at the time? Some, no doubt. But that's a serious commitment, and to me it meant they had *made it*.

Of course when you're young you're oblivious to the fact that a move like that means you're now a small fish playing in a very large ocean. But, as the interview reveals, Hoi Polloi went from playing to tens of people in places like Te Awamutu, to literally tens of thousands of people in places like Pennsylvania.

They saw both ends of the spectrum in terms of success, such as having only ten dollars to share between them at one point, to earning tens of thousands of dollars from some of their more lucrative gigs.

Magazine cover photo shoots? Check. Screaming fans? Check. Band masseur? Check. (What the?) But – and I'll use Jenny's expression here – 'Boy howdy' don't think for a minute that all that stuff lingers the most in their collective memories.

I met the band in Auckland at the home of Derek Lind's manager (Steve 'Albert' Hamilton and his wife Cheryl), as it was a good central point for the band to meet. It didn't take long for the early afternoon to turn into evening as we talked about the old days. Ladies and gentlemen, meet the first New Zealand Christian band to sign an international record deal... Hoi Polloi.

Brett Wilson: When was the last time you were all together in the same room?

Jozsef Fityus (drums): We've failed these last 12 months, but for the last two or three years we've tried to get together every month and do this [hang out together]. And we occasionally pick up our instruments, and that's our 'Book Club' really.

Dave Ball (guitar): Yeah, we have a 'Book Club!' We've tried to write quite a few songs. We're full of riffs and we've got lots and lots of stuff, fresh material, but we can never finish anything. [Laughter]

Jozsef: We have short attention spans!

Andrew Horst (bass): Young people today, eh? [Laughter]

Jenny Horst (nee Gullen) (vocals/guitar): We are challenged with very busy lives and it's not often that we can get together.

Jozsef: [The reunion] was the result of Parachute Festival approaching us back in 2009. They were doing a retrospective; I can't remember why...

Everyone else: The 20th anniversary of Parachute Festival.

Jozsef: We were invited to play, and we hadn't up until that point, since returning from the US. There were 16 or 17 years where we hadn't hung out at all.

BW: Apparently the band went by the name of Jamboree before it was Hoi Polloi, but a short clip of Jamboree online reveals a fairly different line-up. Was Jamboree a different band?

Jozsef: It goes back before that. A super-brief history: I moved from the Waikato to Auckland with my parents and started going to Ranui Baptist and met Dave Ball. He had an acoustic guitar and I had a motocross bike. We went to CTC [Capital Teen Convention] and it literally changed my life.

Dave: Opened your eyes, eh?

Jozsef: It did, yeah. And I met Perry Bradley [who later married Jozsef's sister Belinda] and Jeff Tribe and a few other guys on the bus on the way down [to Wellington]. Got back and went, 'We're gonna start a band!' It was as black and white as that. So I traded my motocross bike for a drum kit, and you were learning classical guitar at the time?

Dave: Yeah, classical.

Jozsef: Because we couldn't play anybody else's songs, we started writing our own songs. That morphed into Standing Joke, because people kind of left but it was Dave and I and Belinda and Perry and...

Dave: Jeff...

Jozsef: ...at some stage you became the bass player.

Andrew: Yeah, I was a temporary guy that had to play because your regular guy was a little bit irregular... the regular guy.

Dave: Yeah... bass players are like that. [Laughter]

Andrew: They said, 'We need to get a permanent guy. Can you help us out and come and learn some songs?' So I did, and they said, 'Oh, that's really good! Are you available?' And I said, 'Sure. Tell me when you want me.' And apparently the other bass player said, 'Oh, you've got another bass player? Oh, sweet! I can go and do my own thing now!' So I became a permanent member. Then I went overseas for an O.E. for four months, and Jozsef sent me a letter...

Dave: An actual letter!

Andrew: ...and he said, 'How you going? Good news and bad news. Bad news first: the band split up. The good news: we've got another guitar player and a singer, and a spot's open for you when you come back.' I was like, 'Oh, sweet! That sounds good!' I think you already had a name by the time I got back.

Jozsef: Didn't we go with Hoi Polloi, then Jamboree?

Jenny: It started as Hoi Polloi and changed to Jamboree, and it wasn't until I joined that it went back to Hoi Polloi.

Jozsef: Jamboree was the three of us [Dave, Andrew and Jozsef] and Dave 'Steiny' Steunebrink on guitar and Brent Tasker on vocals. We had a little bit of secular success. We did a demo and Jayrem Records in Wellington got hold of it and said, 'This is amazing. We want you to do an EP.'
Colin Hogg reviewed it as one of the Top 10 releases of 1985. Then after that we did a gig at Galaxy, which is now the Powerstation, and Paul Ellis [Sony Music] saw us and signed us

to Hit Singles for a second EP. And then, like all bands, things morph and Brent went to... where did he go?

Andrew: Australia. Brisbane.

Jozsef: And we were left looking for a singer.

Dave: We auditioned this one here [Jenny].

Jozsef: Jenny came along and we all went, 'Ah ha!'

Andrew: I had the final say. Because these guys were all engaged to be married and um... I wasn't. [Laughter] But she did have singing qualities to befit the standard necessary, eh darl? [Laughter]

BW: One might expect you'd be looking for a new singer who sounded similar to your old singer.

Jozsef: I think initially we thought that was very true, but when Jenny came along we just went, 'Well actually, we don't need to be tied to that [sound].'

Jenny: There was a purposeful shift in sound as well because obviously I learned the songs that Brent had written the melodies and lyrics for, but we began adding new material that we co-created. There was a decision to shift the sound a little bit; that it was okay to do that. As Jozsef said, we weren't beholden to what was; this was a new chapter in the story and we could explore a new sound.

BW: Is there a date or a year when Hoi Polloi became an official thing?

Dave: Probably when Steiny left.

Jenny: Well, 1988 was when I joined the band. Steiny was in the band as the second guitarist, playing rhythm for another year probably. Then he left and I picked up my guitar...

Jozsef: He didn't leave the band; he actually left his position.

Jenny: He said he wanted to become the manager of the band, which came out of left-field. But we all agreed that it would be amazing because we were starting to get interest and getting very busy.

We were rehearsing three nights a week and playing at least one night a week, usually two. So it was a major commitment and there were opportunities coming our way, and so to have someone navigate that for us was very helpful. We had Ross Inglis before that. He did a superb job but he was no longer available. Steiny was attracted to that role and did a great job of it too.

BW: So things started to happen for the band because of the management?

Jenny: Um... it was a combination, I think. We were beginning to refine our sound...

Jozsef: It takes a while to do that.

Jenny: ...and develop a core set of pretty good songs. The catalyst for the major leap to the States was playing at Shelterbelt.

Jozsef: I look back to 30 years ago, and we had a pretty amazing work ethic. I mean we all had full-time jobs, we had young families and all that stuff going on, but there was a commitment to actually practising three times a week and playing sometimes twice a weekend. I'm not sure if you see that these days.

I mean, I think what's happening today is that you've got young people that get really good really quickly. They start playing when they're 10 or 11 or 12 and by the time they're 15 or 16 they're phenomenal, and there's no reason why New Zealand musicians, both Christian and mainstream, couldn't be making better in-roads. But I think the Millennial thing is a real thing; a lack of work ethic. But I'm sounding like an old man.

BW: Well, we've had a whole spat of talent shows where people are stars overnight. Plus, people rely on their online presence a lot these days, for exposure. But rather, you guys were gigging or at least practising three nights a week.

Jenny: Also, outside of that you're working on your songwriting. I think there probably wasn't any day of the week where I wasn't writing by myself at home. The other part of the dynamic was that the New Zealand music scene was very different at the time.

There were very few signed bands, and few New Zealand bands played on the radio, so it was dominated by international music. Record labels here were basically marketing what was provided to them internationally. They weren't scouring clubs and pubs for the hot new thing. I guess there wasn't really a market for New Zealand music quite so much.

Andrew: Outside of the powerhouses and the bands we all knew about, it stayed like that for a long time.

Jenny: Yeah. It was a very static music scene and so for us crafting original music and working as hard as we did and being somewhat ambitious was quite unusual. Would that be true Jozsef?

Jozsef: Well, it's a biased viewpoint. I'd agree. But if you try and step back from the whole thing, there was a vital live thing going on. Not a lot of recording or radio airplay but there were more venues back then than there are today.

Andrew & Dave: Good venues!

Jozsef: Great P.A.s, great lighting.

Jenny: But when we were overseas the whole market changed rapidly and significantly. We came back five years later to a New Zealand music scene that was very different and starting to be quite vibrant and really embraced by New Zealanders. So we kind of missed that lift in the market here in New Zealand.

Andrew: We were in cringe factor state still.

BW: The cultural cringe factor?

Jenny: Yeah, it really was. I think people called us the most well-known unsigned band in New Zealand at one stage.

BW: A common theme that has emerged with the musos I've interviewed for this book is the influence of other musicians, whether they be Christian or mainstream artists. This is interesting because we're talking about a time when many Christians were encouraged to listen to Christian music and to avoid

Let's Back Up a Bit

secular music. This is something that has waned over the years from my observation. So with all of that in mind, who were some of your influences?

Andrew: We were talking about Capital Teen Convention before. I remember going to those conventions as a young fulla, 11 or 12 years old. I used to live in Wellington so I'd go to that. I'd just be watching these bands and singers and artists every year. I was pretty loyal to it and I loved it!

BW: Do you remember any particular artists that made an impression?

Andrew: No! I can't remember anyone. Oh... well I remember her! [Points to Jenny. Laughter]

BW: So one time you went and Jenny was there?

Andrew: Yeah. I would've been about 16 or 17 then.

BW: And little did you know then that you would marry her one day. When did you get married?

Jenny: 1990.

BW: So you spent two years together in the band before you got married?

Jenny: Yeah. And the band was the reason we had children so late in our marriage, too.

BW: Influences, Dave?

Dave: My earliest influences in the Christian field were Phil Keaggy and Larry Norman and a few others. I saw Phil Keaggy play electric guitar and that was my first realisation that electric guitar might be pretty cool. But then I saw him play all of this classical stuff and I thought, 'That looks pretty cool too.' So I started getting into classical guitar after that and did well with that.

Andrew: He did *very* well, actually.

Dave: But later on, as I grew up, I started listening to more music outside of Christian music. We actually played some gigs with people like Simple Minds. We supported them once. Remember that?

Jozsef: Oh... it was so long ago... I should remember this.

Andrew: It was in Main Street.

Jozsef: I *do* remember!

BW: Jamboree opened for Simple Minds?

Jozsef: It would've been Standing Joke.

Dave: And U2 of course, they were quite influential, particularly the *Boy* album.

BW: I remember you guys playing a song from the *War* album.

Jozsef: 'Seconds'.

Let's Back Up a Bit

Jenny: Mmm. We almost opened for them later on, didn't we?

A discussion takes place as to when this happened, how many times it happened, whether it coincided with the funeral of U2's roadie, Greg Carroll, oh... and the time Bono quoted Hoi Polloi lyrics from the stage as part of an ad-lib moment.

Jenny: He [Bono] sang some of the lines from our song 'Rest Tonight' during one of their songs at Western Springs in 1989. We were in the audience, gasping in disbelief! We narrowly missed out on opening for them so I guess it was a little nod to us! But we did open for Amy Grant. [Chuckling from other band members]

We toured Australia with her in 1991 for her *Heart in Motion* tour. It was a real mismatch.

Jozsef: Big arenas. 12,000 seats. That sort of thing. And to maximise the impact, we'd do the Amy gig, pack everything up, and go to a club or a bar and do a second show.

Dave: We did too!

Jozsef: That's a work ethic!

BW: I think the work ethic of the band separated you guys from a lot of other bands on the scene. If I can share my own insight, I was in an acoustic duo called Holy Smoke and we opened for you guys at a gig in Te Awamutu and...

Jozsef: I remember that gig!! I remember that one!!

BW: That's the one you remember?! You struggle to remember opening for Simple Minds, but you remember a little gig in Te Awamutu?! [Laughter]

SPAMM magazine informs me that this gig was on September 13, 1991.

I think it was Holy Smoke, the Revs and Hoi Polloi. I would've been 17 years old and my impression of you guys was just a really polished act. You might as well have been U2 as far as I was concerned. I was young but I'm sure a lot of people felt the same way. There was obviously some intention on your part in terms of a real work ethic. Had you talked about it as a band?

Jenny: Well, I have a philosophy that if you're going to do something you may as well do it the best you can and make the most of the opportunity in front of you. I think we all felt we had something special going on. There was a musical and relational chemistry that worked between us; we really enjoyed each other.

But there was a sound that we had that was a little different, and I guess we figured that often it's the details that make the difference. It's how one song leads into another, it's how you set the stage up, it's the look, it's the ambience, it's the music that's playing before you get on stage, it's the communication between songs, it's the way you move on stage, it's refining those interesting little elements in the song that create a change or a new dynamic, it's leveraging the uniqueness in the band, which for us, a lot of it hinged on Dave's amazing guitar work...

Dave: Crafting our look as well. There was a certain look about what we did. The shoes we wore, the clothes we put on. We thought about all of that.

Jozsef: We've ridden this last 35 years together, off and on, and we know each other really well which is an amazing thing when you stop and think about it. And every person in this band, I know their hearts and their intentions, there are no prima donnas and I mean that genuinely. So I don't want this to come across from a place of 'Look at us!'

But I don't know if we knew where we were going or where we wanted to go. I think there was a sense that we could do something. Whether there was an element of blind ambition? I think every artist needs an amount of tunnel vision to achieve what they wanna achieve. I mean it's really hard to talk to, to be honest, because we did what we did instinctively. It wasn't out of a book. It wasn't like, 'Here's the manual. Do it this way.'

Jenny: The international stage was not even featuring in our minds at all because in New Zealand at the time, no bands were getting signed internationally...

Jozsef: Not in Te Awamutu anyway! [Laughter] In some ways there was a sense of naivety and ridiculous brashness because the bands at the time – there was Derek [Lind] and Darlene and Kevin [Adair] – were way better musicians to be fair. I mean my drumming never passed journeyman stage, ever. Dave's unique in terms of his sound and Andrew's a great bass player. But something happened collectively that you can't magic up. You'd know that with your own musical endeavours.

BW: Sure.

Dave: Do you remember the Crystal Palace gigs? Before the Shelterbelt gig? Kevin Adair's organisation, Someone Up There, organised these gigs. It really generated a lot of forward momentum for Hoi Polloi I think. I remember there were 700 people crammed in this place and we came on and there was this big surge of people, the whole crowd went whoosh!

BW: So was that a moment where you thought, 'Wow. Something is happening here.'

Dave: It was, yeah.

Jenny: Yeah, there was not only an impetus or momentum within the band to keep striving forward and to achieve the next thing and to better what we were doing at every point, but at the same time there was momentum from the other side, from the audience that was growing and becoming more loyal and impassioned about the music that we were creating. So there was a lot of energy meeting in the middle that kind of spurred us all on, I suppose.

BW: Any influences on you Jenny, especially vocally?

Jenny: I was listening to a lot of Pat Benatar and Melissa Etheridge. They were the edgiest females I could find at the time. They had a lot of angst, a lot of honesty. Mining the depth of emotion type thing. I did listen to Christian music but I didn't find what I was looking for as far as female vocalists that I wanted to emulate.

BW: It's hard to find a good *rock* voice from a female. In my experience in music education, it's a pretty rare thing.

Jenny: It's an interesting thing. I think there's the challenge as a Christian woman, particularly in cultures like the US where it can be a little sheltered and conservative, the notion of being edgy on stage in terms of performance or vocal delivery or lyrics.

I don't mean morally edgy lyrics, but just being kind of raw and real. My approach was a little bit out of step with a lot of what they were doing over there, so I can understand what you're saying. It's more likely to be conservative and that's the expectation.

So for us, when we arrived in the States, there were a lot of people who said, 'Oh! Thank goodness! This is something that we've been looking for, for a long time.' This was from the punters, the fans that were pretty keen to see this alternative rock thing starting out that we were a part of. That was somewhat new.

I shared a snippet from the band's entry in the Encyclopedia of Contemporary Christian Music, which states that the band's success, according to CCM magazine, had more to do with Jenny's appearance and personality than the band's musical ability.

Andrew: That's why I married her mate! [Laughter]

BW: Was that a common barrier? The fact that you, Jenny, were – especially for the time – a woman in a so-called 'man's world'.

Jenny: Oh, well, there were other women around.

BW: But were you taken just as seriously as a frontman might've been?

Jenny: Oh, in rock music there probably weren't that many women. But I didn't feel like I wasn't taken seriously to be honest.

That's the first time I've heard that kind of comment. I think the general consensus was that the sound of the band was incredibly fresh and the energy we brought to the stage ... so yeah, I think that would stand for itself.

As a woman on stage in the Christian world, I think there was the barrier of wearing clothes that I felt were kind of cool, but conservative audiences thought they were a bit edgy. So there were times where they would have a quiet word, 'You can't wear that.'

PHOTO CREDIT: MARK TUCKER.

Andrew: 'You might wanna put a dress on!'

Jenny: [Laughter]

Dave: Did they say that?!

Jenny: Yeah. You get judged more quickly and they'd assume things and um...

BW: Judged more quickly than a male would?

Jenny: Oh, generally it wasn't a problem.

Jozsef: [After selecting the photo on this page] You see, for the time, there was nobody in CCM that looked like that. Seriously.

Let's Back Up a Bit

BW: I guess if it was an issue you would've felt frustration towards people who were concentrating on other things, as opposed to your art.

Jenny: Well, I was on the cover of magazines and sometimes I got told off for having my skirts too short and things like that, but it was normal to me, and in mainstream culture no one would've blinked an eye. I was just me. I tried to be responsible. I tried to be my creative self. I like to have fun.

I didn't try to be purposely provocative other than in our music. I suppose it's a fine line when you're a woman on stage and people wanna make certain judgments. But I honestly think the music was the primary thing that people were interested in and that was certainly the feedback we were getting.

BW: Fair enough. Influences on you Jozsef?

Jozsef: I remember hearing *Boy* by U2 and thinking, 'Crikey. That's pretty stunning.' That era, the early '80s, is much copied and emulated now but there was some amazing stuff like the Waterboys and the Blue Nile and Talk Talk, and there were all these alt-British guitar bands doing this incredible stuff.

BW: Many of the bands you've mentioned are secular. Did you battle with the idea that this was seen by some as the devil's music or was that not an issue?

Jozsef: Not really, no.

Dave: We were conscious of it.

Andrew: It's partly to do with how you were brought up. For me, I'm not saying my dad was 'out there' by any stretch of the imagination, but he would have a Doobie Brothers' album or other stuff that was very contemporary like a Paul Simon album. And he loved playing it.

He was a very conservative Dutch Christian man with otherwise very conservative views, but his music tastes were quite varied, and so I thought, 'Well if it's alright for him to listen to that, then I can to listen to maybe a bit of Peter Frampton or um... certainly not the Rolling Stones.' [Laughter]

Jozsef: It's such a big question and it has plagued Christendom forever, whether it's music or art or whatever it is. I think it's a distraction to a degree. Is it God's music or the devil's music? It's not the answer and it's not even the question.

I think we've all been drawn towards stuff that's *authentic*. Now the authenticity might be coming from a dark place, but you recognise the authenticity when you hear it. It doesn't mean you embrace the lifestyle, but you actually appreciate it for what it is.

Most Christian music is too prescriptive. It's like if you try to please everybody all the time you miss the boat, and you've actually got to be a bit myopic and single-minded and go, 'This is what we're trying to achieve with the abilities that we have.' And if you do that, and stay true to that, then the chances are you will come up with something that is worthy of something.

It might not sell many records but... it really depends on your world view. If you take popular culture, you take hip-hop culture, rock culture, the excesses and the hedonism of all that stuff from a Christian perspective, the devil has grabbed hold of it and used that through various subversive channels and has marketed that to distract and destroy people. No question. That's not even an argument. But do you then throw all art out?

Let's Back Up a Bit

Dave: Exactly.

Jozsef: You can't! Because creativity is God-given and God isn't about saccharine and sweet and homogenised. He's about the light and the dark and He's about the tension that exists between the two. It's about falling and redemption; it's all of that... sorry I'm on a bit of a...

Andrew: No, no! It's good!

Dave: Go for it Joe!

Jozsef: As Christians, whether you're an artist or not, we get side-tracked by the wrong argument. You've got to be able to separate that out and kind of go, 'God is in all of this [secular art].' Yes, the people who are creating it may be oblivious to the concept of God or have rejected God's plan for their lives. It doesn't mean that their output isn't worthy of something. Because they're driven to create – which is instilled into them by a Creator.

They'll be at odds with themselves. There'll be conflict, because they kind of know – somewhere we all kind of know – that tension. But sometimes I think God is closer to *those* people than He is to the pious.

Jenny: And that plays out in Scripture pretty clearly, doesn't it? In the Gospels. We found ourselves in the deepest, darkest pubs and clubs in New Zealand and overseas that the average Christian band wouldn't have been able to darken the doorstep of.

They wouldn't have wanted to or have had the opportunity to. But the conversations that would spark up in those environments after we've played were pretty amazing. People would open up to us in quite profound ways. Not because our music was overtly Christian at all, but it did speak from a deep place that was authentic, that was full of imagery and alluded to things spiritual and this rich relationship we have with God.

So we talked to people about their issues around struggling with suicide or grief or whatever they were going through. Pretty amazing opportunities. So just being real wherever you are, and being what you're called to be, which for us wasn't a wearing-it-all-on-your-sleeve, evangelical band; it was being true to ourselves and what we were called to be.

Dave: Oh, we did experiment with backward masking though! [Laughter]

Jenny: On the second album, eh? On 'Love Shine Down'.

Dave: The notion of backward masking is just ludicrous. We thought, 'We gotta try it out!' So we did and it came out, 'Eeeeoooorrrrrrrr!!!!'

BW: And what was the message?

Dave: No, it was just my guitar! [Laughter] No, we were quite conscious of it, I must say. We were conscious of hypocrisy in CCM too. Just the desire to get quick 'decisions' for the Lord at a gig.

The thing about music that you learn quite early on is that it's really emotive, and you're able to control emotions really easily and to be able to link an emotion with a thought or a theme. So the responsibility was on us to actually portray things in a much better light.

Talking about some difficult things sometimes can actually

need angry music, and a really good worship song can actually be … like our song 'Take Me Home'. Sometimes when we played that one there would be incredible worship on stage. I remember one time in Texas this church was just going off and the pastor came up to me and said, 'That was the most amazing worship I've had in my life.' I'm thinking, 'What was that about?'

BW: And that song doesn't even mention Jesus or anything like that.

Jenny: No. But we would pray before every gig. I mean, our spiritual lives were really alive and vibrant. We really felt we were bringing something that was meaningful and wanted God to use that to bring life and hope.

BW: Were you ever confronted by people who questioned what you were doing?

All of a sudden looks are exchanged between the band as they seemed to think of the same incident all at once. This is quickly followed by comments such as 'Should we tell that story?' 'Yeah! Tell the story!' The band eventually decide on where the story should start and whether it involved CCM superstars, Holy Soldier or Guardian.

Jenny: We were touring with Guardian and we'd just driven 16 hours to a gig. We get there and we're starting to load in…

Andrew: We're carrying the P.A. for the bands because we had a big trailer. The road crew turns up and says, 'Oh, what stuff is this? Is this Guardian's stuff?'

Hoi Polloi: 'Nah, this is our stuff.'

Crew: 'Oh, okay. Where's the P.A.?'

Hoi Polloi: 'Well, it's all coming out after our band gear.'

Crew: 'No, we're just unloading the P.A.'

Hoi Polloi: 'Oh, why is that?'

Crew: 'We can't say. We're just unloading the P.A.'

Hoi Polloi: 'Oh. Is the promoter here?'

Crew: 'Yeah.'

Promoter: 'Yeah, we need to have a chat.'

Hoi Polloi: 'Sorry?'

Promoter: 'Yeah, we're just gonna set up the P.A. and let Guardian do their thing.'

Hoi Polloi: 'Oh, okay. Great. Cool, let's have a chat then.'

Andrew: And apparently...

Jenny: They said, 'You can't play.' And we said, 'Oh. Why? Is there a change of plan? We've just driven 16 hours. Is Guardian not able to play or...'

Promoter: 'No, Guardian can play, but you can't play. There's a problem.'

Let's Back Up a Bit

Jenny: It took us ages to find out what the jolly problem was. We were saying, 'Well, what is the problem?' They said, 'We can't say.' We're like, 'Well, we probably should know. We'd like to know what this problem is.'

We're thinking, 'Gosh, what's happened?' It took us probably half an hour for them to talk about the problem. They eventually disclosed that we were clearly not a band with any integrity because they had seen...

Andrew: Me.

Jenny: ...someone they knew had seen Andrew having a beer at a showcase event in Nashville...

Andrew: A *Christian* showcase.

Dave: It was an after-party thing... in a pub!

Jenny: And the beer was given to him by our record label executive...

Andrew: A *Christian* record label executive.

Jenny: It was one beer but, for them, for a Christian to drink alcohol was a...

Jozsef: A deal breaker.

Dave: The irony was everyone in that room was drinking alcohol and they were all Christians.

Andrew: So as the promoter is explaining this to us, we're sitting there looking incredulous. But he's taking this as a sign of repentance. But actually we were thinking, 'We can't believe you're having this conversation with us!' [Laughter]

Jenny: We had also been blacklisted from the local Christian radio stations for the same reason.

Andrew: So he said, 'Oh well, okay. We can see that you're sorry for what you did and we'll let you play now.'

Jenny: There was the odd occasion like that and there was the odd interview on a Christian radio station where I would apparently swear, but I did not know that it was a swear word...

Andrew: 'Crap' is a swear word!

Jenny: They would say, 'I can't believe you just said that!' So you just stumble over cultural differences or differences within the Christian cultures of the States as well. What was permissible and what wasn't could be very different.
    In some places we went to, the kids weren't allowed to dance. If they did dance they would be fined $50 at a Christian college or something. We had a mix of gigs. We did see quite a diverse array of promoters and contexts and audiences. We were playing in clubs as well as in Christian colleges...

Dave: Festivals.

Andrew: Street festivals.

Jenny: So secular and Christian contexts, and being the same band in all of it, to be fair.

Let's Back Up a Bit

BW: So let's talk about your journey to the USA and how you got there.

Jenny: So we played at Shelterbelt Festival in Te Puke in 1989. Rez Band was the headline act and they saw us play and they said, 'Hey, we run this alternative rock festival in Chicago called Cornerstone. We think you'd go down well there. Could you come along?' So we turned up there in 1990…

Andrew: We had cassettes of our demo but we didn't have the covers so, because Jenny was in the design industry, she worked all night the night before the festival designing and printing cover sleeves, so we had a product to sell.

Jenny: That's right. We turned up on stage, it was a big stage and it was a large crowd, a few thousand…

Jozsef: We were opening for David Mullen.

Jenny: And he was late…

Dave: His flight was cancelled or something…

Jozsef: He didn't turn up.

Jenny: Right. So we got extra time, which was brilliant. But nothing seemed to go well from my perspective. My guitar lead wasn't working, there were sound issues, the foldback wasn't quite what it needed to be. So we were on stage feeling quite frustrated, but the audience was absolutely lighting up and on fire and there was huge energy there…

Jozsef: It went off.

Jenny: It did go off. So basically, for whatever reason, despite the issues we were having, the gig really took off and according to reviews of Cornerstone Festival it was cited as the standout moment of the festival.

Dave: Crazy eh? Because they have massive big bands there.

Jenny: Oh, they had huge names there. The biggest names in the country went there to play.

Dave: It was the first time we got introduced to the whole media frenzy thing. We went back to this large caravan and had microphones in front of us and all these people wanted to interview us.

Jozsef: Yeah, and we had this bidding war. Literally, after we got off stage, we had six record companies lined up ready to sign us. It was just bizarre. So we spent the next year talking to a whole bunch of labels, and I think we dismissed the first lot pretty quickly and it got down to Word and Reunion, and they sent their respective A&R [Artist and Repertoire] people back to New Zealand to hang out for a couple of weeks.

Jenny: And they wooed us. [Laughter]

Jozsef: Well they both did... but we should've gone the other way... anyway. [Laughter]

Dave: Should've gone with Word.

Jenny: They were both good options, but in the end we went with Reunion. It was the start of something. I remember after a gig around that same time at a club in Nashville someone in the industry said, 'I've seen the future of Christian music, and it's from New Zealand.'

BW: Wow. Did you ever think about signing with a secular label?

Andrew: The offers came from Christian labels.

Jozsef: The attraction to Reunion was that they had mainstream distribution through [secular label] Geffen and that was their carrot.

Jenny: But we didn't entertain the idea of a secular label being interested in us, it was more like, 'Far out! These labels wanna sign us!' So we just talked with whoever was in front of us.

I don't know what you guys think, but we probably thought that might be a bit outside of our reach to sign with a secular label. But in retrospect it might've been a good thing to actually scope that out a bit more, and see where we fitted best.

I think, for us, one of the challenges with the US experience was that the whole Cornerstone thing filtered our thinking for quite a while because we were thinking, 'Wow. We've obviously got something that people are looking for, audiences are responding to us, there's a niche for us here, we can do something meaningful and rewarding in this space and be ourselves, we're not being asked to change.'

But the challenge for us once we moved to the States and after we recorded our first album, was that it was clear Cornerstone was one experience within a very big playing field, and there were a lot of other dynamics that meant that wasn't indicative of the reception we got everywhere we went.

The Cornerstone experience wasn't representative of the *whole* market, so it was a lot more challenging than we thought. So probably, if we'd understood that the Christian music industry was a bit more conservative than we realised, we would have scoped out some other options in the secular market.

Jozsef: There was a naivety there.

Jenny: We had absolutely nobody guiding us as well, which is one of my big regrets. Perhaps not a regret because I had no control over it at the time, but it wasn't an age where you sought out mentors.

At this stage in my life, I know that when someone has an opportunity, there are any number of people they can go to and seek advice. They can get mentors and coaching and wisdom imparted to help them navigate what's in front of them.

For us, we were called trailblazers because no one else had done it before us – but there was nobody we even thought of asking 'What do we do here?' I mean there was the odd pastor or father we might ask, I guess, but they didn't know. How could they navigate what was in front of us that was a whole other world and culture?

BW: Band management wasn't guiding you?

Jozsef: Yeah, but our manager was our friend and he was going through the same motions we were, you know? Discovering stuff at the same time we were.

Jenny: In retrospect, how amazing it would've been if someone had been in that role, either US-based or wherever, just to say, 'Hey guys, this is the nature of the industry. Here's some of what you'll encounter, here's some good advice and this is what you should be looking for and don't sign too soon and da-de-da-de-da.'

Jozsef: But the reality is that commercial success in the Christian music industry in the early '90s in America meant compromise. Good songs? Sure. But more than that was actually placating your audience and giving them exactly what they wanted and – to be quite frank – we weren't prepared to do that.

Jenny: That's beautifully said.

Andrew: And to say all of that, now contemplate all of that before you move *everything you have* and *all that is dear to you* to America... *to live.*

Jenny: We arrived in America with 12 people; the band, wives, children, manager and sound guy. That's a lot of people to feed and house when the band is unknown.

The great mistake we made in the early stages was believing the hype that the next gig was gonna be the biggest thing we'd ever seen, and that we'd make lots of money from selling lots of merchandise and what have you.

We were being fed quite a bit of hype before we arrived and after we arrived as well, so the expectations on earnings was quite unrealistic. What we learned the hard way was that we were an unknown band needing to prove ourselves, and nothing was going to be handed to us on a plate. So we didn't earn much money for a very long time and we developed a debt pretty quickly.

So that hampered us a lot and it meant we weren't as nimble and responsive to opportunities as we could've been if we were financially flush and able to pick and choose strategically what we should do. We followed the money basically so we could get the bills paid and get the people fed.

Jozsef: And you add to that – and this is gonna sound cynical and you take it for what it's worth – but I mean we toured with bands, and I won't name names, that knew exactly how to play the CCM market in quite a cynical way.

You know, to a point where they were dialling it up every night, saying the right things in the right place, selling the right kind of merchandise and it was a very orchestrated thing.

I think they had been at it for so long they assimilated into it and didn't really kind of get it. But for us coming in cold, it was wrong; 'We can't do this. We cannot sell our "wares" to make a living.' It's like Jesus in the Temple with the money changers. That's exactly what it was like, seriously.

So we wouldn't merchandise certain things such as crosses, for example, which is pretty fundamental. We wouldn't say things on rote from the stage. We just said, 'We can't do that because that's dishonest.'

Andrew: And those guys were giving us advice: 'This is what you gotta do. I know you've got no money, so this is what you do. This is the formula and once you do that, you'll be sweet.' Because they wanted us to have what they had. So they were being brotherly in that way.

Jenny: To give it a bit of perspective, it wasn't like Hoi Polloi had a problem with people sharing their faith in an overt way from the stage or whatever. But it was the milking of that and manipulating that in order to appease promoters and get big bucks that was the problem.

Let's Back Up a Bit

Andrew: 'Well, we brought 50 people to the Lord today. This time next year we should get another five grand on top of our fee!'

Jenny: But at the end of the day you stand or fall on your character, so that's what we tried to do. We planned to be in the States for six months but for Andrew and I it turned into five years. For Dave and Jozsef it was a bit shorter than that.

If we had our time over, we would've planned it quite differently and it would've been a lot more successful for us on a number of levels, but at the same time we were extremely successful on certain measures as well.

We were described as one of the top live bands in the Christian music scene, or *the* top. We got a couple of number one hits on the CCM charts, and one of them stayed at the top of the charts for eight weeks or something.

We were nominated for some Dove Awards, *Rock Album of the Year*. That's the Christian equivalent of the Grammys. We charted on College Radio, which is quite an important secular chart for more alternative music. We were played on MTV and we played some amazing gigs as well. It was phenomenal.

Andrew: And just the sort of on-the-ground support and reception we received, that was what encouraged us to stay. Whether it be from people you chatted to, or just their response to you actually playing, or the relationships you formed. There was always hope in that regard. It was like, 'Okay. Let's sit it out. Let's go harder! [Pause] Let's just eat less!' [Laughter]

BW: It's good to hear about your achievements because they're important, but also it can be a bit of an awkward thing to talk about. It's often easier for others to talk about your success.

Jenny: It is actually. One of the strange dynamics, Brett, was that when we came back to New Zealand, it was like walking into a vacuum almost. We no longer had a presence here.

We'd been gone so long and the industry had changed so much, and we've never been able to find our way back in. I mean, we didn't try very hard to be frank. When I came back I was like, 'Okay, I'm stepping out of music for a while.'

BW: You'd had enough?

Jenny: I hadn't had enough of music at all, but we came back to some pretty challenging situations with family members being incredibly ill and so forth, and wanting to quickly try and establish ourselves in work and with income. Music had to take a back seat.

But in the States, certainly in pockets, we were actually quite famous. We were travelling relentlessly – 200 shows a year – and we might turn up to a McDonalds in the middle of nowhere and people would say, 'OH! IT'S HOI POLLOI!' They would be asking for photos and stuff. And a number of times we'd go to a gig and we'd be crowded by people screaming and wanting autographs.

Andrew and I headlined a festival in Brazil to 40,000 people. There was a lot of screaming at that gig. So it was quite fascinating – there was this element of fame overseas, but it hadn't translated to life back here in New Zealand so much. It was almost as though we had another life there and one that was not congruous with the life we have now.

Jozsef: Well, social media didn't exist back then. No one was using the Internet.

BW: You were talking before about certain bands that would do things in the 'right way' because that's what was expected from a Christian band. Did you, Jenny, feel a compulsion or an expectation to give a Christian message in between songs? Did that come naturally to you? I guess another way to ask the same question would be, if you were to do a gig now would you feel compelled to give a Christian message?

Jenny: I'd probably feel more compelled to do it now to be honest, but perhaps not in the normal way. I'd probably focus on matters of social injustice and how we might respond to that, if we dared to follow Jesus' lead.

In Hoi Polloi, there were times where I did speak at length if it was the right context, and we felt moved to do that. But I guess the point of difference was that it wasn't formulaic. It wasn't something we'd trot out because we knew that was a means to more success, it was more that at that point in time, I felt like it was something that needed to be said for this audience.

You've got an incredible platform as a performer. If you've drawn an audience, they're there to listen to you. We always said, 'Well, the songs are saying what we wanna say,' but there is the added opportunity to use that platform to unpack concepts or things that are important, and also for the audience to get to know us as well, which is also quite meaningful for both parties.

These days I'm probably more impassioned about particular issues than I ever was and, boy howdy, if you gave me a stage I'd want to speak about them. I'd probably do it more effectively than I could've in a song, because some of them are quite complex issues and I struggle to write about them.

There were social justice issues in our songs, but these days those things burn on my heart a lot more because of various experiences I've had, and opportunities I've seen to effect change.

BW: When you think back to your time in the US, what stands out the most?

Andrew: Oh, just the cultural experience, 'Look at that! Who would've thought people would do that kind of stuff?'

BW: [Laughter] A great way to see the world!

Andrew: We played in all but three states. The only notable city I don't remember playing in was New Orleans.

BW: So basically you spent a long time in a van.

Jenny: We spent an average of eight hours a day in a van.

For the next ten minutes the band reminisce over certain highlights, which include sunsets in the Rockies, coyotes and bears, various people they met and various accounts of trekking the USA in a 38-foot, 1975 Dodge Motorhome given to them by the Newsboys, which used more oil than it did petrol, had one working brake, broke down several times, caught fire once and, in freezing weather, formed ice on the inside (hence its nickname, 'the Fridge').

BW: It's interesting that the highlights have nothing to do with music. Are you happy to talk about the low lights? What was the lowest point in the band?

Andrew: Ah... when this particular group of four people split up. Looking back on it – the way that it happened – I could've changed that and not let that happen, but I didn't. I wish I had and I'm forever sorry about that and I'm forever grateful to these two gentlemen [Dave and Jozsef] for forgiving me.

BW: What could you have changed?

Andrew: So Steiny came to me after he met with the record company and said, 'We need to do something different, it's not working, there's a five-figure debt, we can't pay for things, and the creativity has stalled. The record company wanna see something new.

We should send the other boys home and get some Americans in instead, let Jenny come to the fore, you're her husband so you can play bass for her.' And I'm like, 'Ah... okay... is that really what you wanna do?'

Jenny: Steiny said that the only way we were going to pay the debt off was for us to pay it off with American dollars, because at that stage the American dollar was worth twice as much as the New Zealand dollar. Otherwise we'd be paying it off for the rest of our lives in New Zealand dollars. So we really needed to up the ante, so we could make some money in America.

Andrew: Well, he presented it as two options. Either way, the final solution, according to him, was that Dave and Joe should go home. I was naïve and probably a bit selfish, and I had already expressed to the group at various times, 'Man, we've got a whole lot of debt and we're not paying our way.'

Jenny: We were all pretty scared, to be fair, and so we were all in a desperate place. We were still being told there were all these exciting opportunities ahead, but by that stage we weren't too

Hoi Polloi

ANDREW & JENNY HORST WITH NEW BAND MEMBERS, TROY DAUGHERTY & SCOTTY PEARSON.

sure we could actually bank on any of those anymore. So we were almost grasping at straws and thinking about what we could do to pull out of the situation. We were all exhausted and running out of steam emotionally.

Dave: The powerhouse for us was creativity, and we hadn't been creative for a while.

Let's Back Up a Bit

BW: What was the thinking behind sending Jozsef and Dave back to New Zealand?

Andrew: Oh, I guess just getting the costs down.

Dave: We also weren't seen as the slickest members of the band.

Andrew: The record company had that point of view.

Jenny: We didn't.

Andrew: And we weren't slick. Nashville was a town of talent like you wouldn't believe. We were a *band*, we weren't a bunch of individuals which Nashville was; a bunch of individuals with talent to boot. So that was their solution to this multi-faceted problem.

BW: But your replacement drummer, Scotty Pearson, is a Kiwi.

Jenny: Yes, but he was a single guy whereas Dave and Jozsef both had wives and children that the band needed to support financially. Work visas limited us to generating income only through music, so that was tough. Scotty was preferred over an American because Hoi Polloi was well known as a New Zealand band and we didn't want to lose that uniqueness. We knew Scotty and knew he was a skilled drummer. He did a great job but unfortunately after some time, immigration issues meant he had to return to New Zealand. So we recruited an American drummer.

Jozsef: Look, the reality is that for the two-and-a-half years we were there together, we lived in a bubble. We were in each other's pockets 24/7, we were broke and it's interesting that the good times were often the small times, not that we didn't enjoy playing, because we did.

But you get to a point where cabin fever sets in and none of us were immune to clouded thinking at all. Man, [to Andrew] you say you regret that and I appreciate you saying that and that's actually the very first time I've heard it kind of couched that way, which is amazing. But we were *all* in a place where we couldn't see the forest for the trees. Seriously.

Jenny: It was no problem for Steiny to bring a scenario to us. We were probably pretty open to all kinds of options and he was absolutely adamant; 'This is it. This is the only thing we can do.'

But the problem was he brought it to Andrew and I – and not to the group – and it's been a profound learning curve in my life and something that has changed a fundamental way that I work with people. These days, if a decision is about a person, it needs to be made *with* that person.

Because Dave and Joe were in it as much as we were. We had no more ownership of Hoi Polloi, we had no more control of it than they did, so the option should've been raised within the group and we all should've debated it and wrestled with it. It would've been uncomfortable for all of us in different ways, and maybe other options could've been brought to the table and we could've explored that together, but that didn't happen.

So then it becomes this weird power dynamic and genuine pain and, for me, that was one of the most painful experiences in my life. It will always be something that I wish had been done differently and, yeah, it's shaped the way that I think and do now, a lesson born out of great pain, and certainly for Dave and Jozsef it was a horrible time.

Andrew: And it was played out over quite a while. We actually did the Guardian tour together after all of that had been done.

Dave: Well, we didn't know that. Is that right? Because the Guardian tour was great. I remember I was wrestling with, 'What is the point of all of this?' and I was really searching God about it. 'What is the one thing You wanna say, Lord, to this generation, through us?'

That was the revelation that came to me; it was about needing to spend time with the Lord, like a bride to a bridegroom, you know? I didn't really see the point anymore after that Guardian tour. Because financially we became a little bit more certain. Some great friendships developed with those Guardian guys. But at the end of that we got back to Nashville and that was the end of Hoi Polloi... well, as we knew it.

Jozsef: Hearing Andrew put it the way he has now ... it was never explained like that to me. They were desperate times, and it was hard for everybody for various reasons. I think one of the biggest disappointments – and it's a past disappointment now – is that very rarely in life do you have a close circle of friends... [emotional pause] that mean as much.

So music aside, there are moments in life that you experience with people, that other people don't get to journey with you in the normal world. So to be cut off from that for a time was the most painful thing. Not the band stuff. That was gonna do whatever it was or wasn't gonna do.

But, what I can say, is that for quite a few years now that's been put right and there's been a healing that's gone on among this group of people, and you are some of the closest and dearest people that I know.

Jenny: Yeah, that's true. One of the great lessons that came out of that experience, apart from the one I mentioned, was: people come first. Before we were about to leave for the States and about to make an important decision with record labels, I felt God say, 'Your love for one another is more important than anything else.' I was like, 'Yeah! Of course we love each other.'

But it's not until the journey is intense and incredibly challenging that love for the people you're journeying with, in whatever context, is tested. There was also the element of, 'We're on a mission from God!' Like the *Blues Brothers*. So in that moment of decision, I'm thinking, 'Well, if the mission is the most important thing and stuff's not making that work, then maybe that stuff's not supposed to be there.'

What I failed to see is actually our primary mission is to love God and to love others around us. We're measured only on those two things in life, when we get to heaven; 'How much did you love Me? How much did you love your neighbour?' And that sometimes means sacrifice. It means patience. It means walking together.

There's an African saying, 'If you want to go fast, go alone. If you want to go far, go together.' For me, that learning was birthed out of that very painful experience, because I realised after the fact that I was primarily called to love these guys and we were all struggling together.

If we had a little bit of wise counsel, we could've possibly wrestled our way out the situation in a way that protected our friendship and was honouring to one another. And I talk about this to this very day, whether it's advice to another band or in a work context, I will say, 'There's nothing more important than what's going on between you all. That's the measure of your faith and your integrity and your love. Hold the mission very lightly because, at the end of the day, your faithfulness to God and the way you treat each other is more important.'

Ultimately, anyone can do the mission. God can call somebody else to do that particular mission if He wants to. It's difficult when people hold things tightly and say, 'This is mine. God's given this to me. I've gotta do it come hell or high water, no matter how much of a trail of destruction is left behind me.'

It's very hard for that ship to change direction when God wants to blow on the sails and say, 'Hey guys, over here now. There's a step-change.' Or, 'Leave that now. I've got something else for you to do.'

That tends to be the way I do my life now. I hold things lightly and search to know whether I've done the right thing by the people around me. I don't always get that right because I'm human and flawed and don't always see things from all angles, but... I'm trying.

Jenny and Andrew eventually returned to New Zealand in 1997. There was major secular label interest in the band in the US at the time, and 18 months later a label was still chasing Jenny for a solo deal.

'We walked away,' says Jenny. 'Andrew felt worn out by life in the US and I wouldn't go back without him. It's taken years to fully appreciate what we experienced together. We're so grateful.'

Today the former Hoi Polloi members work in various jobs in Auckland where they live with their families. Hoi Polloi still get together occasionally to write and individually they play for other friends in live gigs and recording sessions.

OUTRO

These are a few of our homegrown stories from Aotearoa, New Zealand. This is part of my history and perhaps part of yours, too.

For me it was a Christian upbringing that – along with great parents and family and a decent church – provided spiritual food, and I'm grateful for the music I was exposed to in my formative years.

Most of the Bible verses I can recall either come from the songs I blasted on my tape deck or sang in church, usually from the Scripture in Song books.

I sincerely hope the younger generation aren't missing out here; specifically in regard to Scripture in worship music. In their attempts to 'sing a new song to the Lord', modern lyricists often avoid utilising Scripture in favour of a more 'creative' expression. Some songs do this well, but, if this trend continues, then it is possible for Scripture to become separate from worship music.

These days I don't often listen to what is typically classed as 'Christian music', aside from when I'm feeling nostalgic, or when I attend church. As discussed within these chapters, the label 'Christian music' is problematic and hard to define. The discerning feature must be the lyrics; as music (chords, melodies and rhythms) is neither 'Christian' nor 'secular'.

Let's Back Up a Bit

Worship music is designed for a Christian context; primarily, to be sung or played in church. But the music is often no different to love songs played on the radio.

To play the devil's advocate – but certainly not the devil's music – what if the lyrics don't contain any kind of message that could be considered 'Christian'? What if there is no mention of Jesus, no call to salvation, or perhaps even... wait for it... *no lyrics*, as is the case for the many instrumental albums by Phil Keaggy, and other Christian musicians?

How then do we label the music? I would hesitate to call it 'non-Christian music' because I don't subscribe to the notion that music, or any artistic endeavour made by a Christian can only look or sound like one thing.

The God I worship is far bigger and greater than any one style of music or art form. An expansive and beautiful universe and all that it encompasses is one example of His limitless creativity.

Each individual human being on the planet is another example of His boundless creativity. There could never be enough styles of music, lyrical themes or works of art to encapsulate the greatness of God.

'Christian music' may well have been an adequate adjective before more and more artists moved outside of the normal confines of what was deemed 'Christian music'. But these days, I personally don't use the terms 'Christian music' or 'non-Christian music'. I just use the term 'Music'.

It seems that Parachute Music also felt this tension. This is the organisation responsible for promoting and nurturing hundreds of Kiwi Christian artists over the last few decades through its record company and the Parachute Music Festival, which grew to become the largest music festival in the Southern Hemisphere.

Outro

In 2015, Parachute successfully lobbied for the renaming of the Best Gospel/Christian Album category in the New Zealand Music Awards, a category they had originally helped to establish 30 years earlier.

Presenting the newly named Best Worship Album award at the 2015 ceremony, director Mark de Jong explained, 'When we started Parachute Music 25 years ago, Kiwi musicians who wanted to express spirituality in their songs had a hard time finding a platform. Over two decades we've seen a change in the environment; spirituality is no longer relegated to a subculture of its own... "Christian" is not a musical genre.'

Parachute's mission is now focussed on 'creating an open, caring space for those in the wider music industry, regardless of their beliefs,' de Jong says. 'We're informed by the gospel tenets of generosity, hospitality and holistic care, but we no longer feel that needs to be attached to an agenda or subculture.'

That is a significant step to make for an organisation that in de Jong's words has been 'the most high-profile entity in New Zealand "Christian music" over the past 30 years.' It also illustrates a shift in some people's views towards the label of 'Christian music'.

Parachute's removal of the 'Christian' category from the New Zealand Music Awards means that any music that is not deemed worship (but is still 'Christian') is now expected to be nominated in the mainstream categories.

Another illustration of this shift: I was in a band called Somersault around the turn of the Millennium. I was a little taken aback when a younger person recently remembered me as a member of 'that worship band'. Worship band? Somersault was not a worship band!

We were trying to be Christian rock stars for goodness' sake! (Yes, actually for the sake of goodness.) But it now makes sense to me that our explicit Christian lyrics rendered the music as 'worship' to a younger person. Interestingly, the term 'Christian music' didn't appear to be part of their vernacular.

Interviewing the musicians featured in this book has been my great privilege and pleasure. What started as an academic research project while I was teaching in the music department at Vision College, soon turned into a project that carried the weight of responsibility of sharing the stories of this talented group of people.

When I left Vision College, I probably could have left this project unfinished. But I felt it was important to get these artists' stories 'out there' for the sake of posterity. I also wanted to acknowledge, not only their many and varied achievements, but also their contribution to the contemporary Christian music scene in New Zealand and internationally during the '70s, '80s, and '90s.

My sincere thanks to the trailblazers profiled in this book. In their own way, these musicians have revealed deeper layers of music, art, and forms of worship that we may not have realised were there before.

They have made us aware, again, that our God is bigger than we might have first imagined.

ABOUT THE AUTHOR

Brett Wilson lives in Hamilton with his wife, son and daughter. He is an active musician and songwriter, playing at bars and restaurants, corporate events, weddings and at Activate Church, the church he grew up in. After nearly 20 years of teaching music at tertiary level, Brett now works as Communications Co-ordinator at CBS, his brother's Hamilton-based health IT company.

BRETT WILSON - SUPPORTING KIWI CHRISTIAN MUSIC SINCE 1991.

www.ingramcontent.com/pod-product-compliance
Lightning Source LLC
Chambersburg PA
CBHW051353290426
44108CB00015B/1995